Steve Parish
PUBLISHING

Amazing Facts about Australian
Insects & Spiders

Text & photography: Patrick Honan

AMAZING FACTS — INSECTS AND SPIDERS
Contents

INTRODUCTION
WHO'S WHO of invertebrates	4
INVERTEBRATE groups	5
AUSTRALIA'S AMAZING insects & spiders	6
WHAT MAKES an insect?	8

INSECTS
BUTTERFLIES — flying jewels	10
MOTHS — night flyers	12
ANTS — activity unlimited	14
BEES — nectar gatherers	15
WASPS — diverse hunters	16
BEETLES — beetle mania	18
FLIES — two-winged acrobats	20
DRAGONFLIES & DAMSELFLIES — wolves on the wing	21
MANTIDS — perfect predators	22
STICK INSECTS — masters of disguise	23
BUGS — super suckers	24
GRASSHOPPERS & CRICKETS — Aussie jumpers	26
OTHER INSECTS — the less-known groups	27
INHERITORS OF THE EARTH — why so many insects?	29
GETTING THROUGH LIFE — insect life cycles	30
INSECTS THAT DISAPPEAR — camouflage	32
THE GREAT PRETENDERS — mimicry	33
LIVING INSIDE OTHERS — parasitism	34
INSECTS HELPING US — beneficial insects	36
THEM VERSUS US — insects & humans	37
MAKING MORE INSECTS — reproduction	38
SENSING THEIR WORLD — insect senses	40
LIVING COLOURS — insect colours	41
GETTING AROUND — locomotion without wings	42
LIFE ON THE WING — locomotion with wings	43
LIVING UNDER WATER — aquatic insects	44
BUILDING A HOME — insect shelters	45

   LIVING IN GROUPS — social insects   **46**
   LIVING WITH OTHERS — mutualism   **47**
   EATING PLANTS — herbivory   **48**
   MAKING MORE PLANTS — pollination   **49**
   ATTACK — predatory insects   **50**
   PROTECTING THEMSELVES — defence mechanisms   **52**
   GETTING THE MESSAGE ACROSS — communication   **54**
   LIVING IN AUSTRALIA — adapting to extremes   **55**
   INSECTS' ENEMIES — natural foes of insects   **56**
   BIG & SMALL — insect size   **57**

SPIDERS & OTHER ARACHNIDS

   WHAT MAKES a spider?   **58**
   CATCHING FOOD — dinner time   **60**
   SPIDER WEBS — silken artistry   **61**
   MYGALOMORPHS — primitive spiders   **63**
   HUNTERS — huntsmen, wolf spiders & others   **64**
   AMBUSHERS — crab spiders, red-backs & others   **66**
   ORB-WEAVERS — champion spinners   **68**
   JUMPING SPIDERS — great leaps, keen eyes   **70**
   OTHER ARACHNIDS — scorpions, mites & others   **71**

OTHER INVERTEBRATES

   CRUSTACEANS — insects of the sea   **72**
   CENTIPEDES & millipedes   **73**
   WORMS — earthworms, leeches & others   **74**
   SLUGS & SNAILS — mollusc minions   **75**

CONSERVATION

   INSECTS & SPIDERS IN DANGER
   — threatened species & conservation   **76**

GLOSSARY   **78**
WEB LINKS & FURTHER READING   **79**
INDEX   **80**

Who's who of invertebrates

Above: Pipturis weevil. Weevils are the largest family of animals on earth.

Insects and spiders belong to an important group of animals called "invertebrates". Invertebrates are simply animals without backbones — and they make up a phenomenal 98% of all animal species. Without them, our living world would simply not survive and the Earth would be a very different place.

Above: Wolf spiders are ferocious, ground-dwelling predators.

the FACTS!

THERE ARE ABOUT 30 different groups (phyla) of animals on Earth. All vertebrates, including fish, frogs, reptiles, birds and mammals belong to the one phylum (Chordata). The other 29 or so groups are all invertebrates.

MOST OF THE INVERTEBRATES we see live on land. However, the first invertebrates came from the sea and the majority of existing groups of invertebrates still live there.

EACH SPECIES is officially identified with a scientific name. Scientific names have two parts (such as *Homo sapiens* for humans), are usually in an old language called Latin and are written in *italics*.

THE TERM "invertebrate" is sometimes used to include all single-celled organisms. These are so numerous and so little studied, however, that it is nearly impossible to tell how many different types exist.

A SMALL GROUP of invertebrates ("sea squirts") possess the precursor to a backbone. This group is the most closely related to the vertebrates.

FILING THEM INTO PHYLA

The largest grouping in the animal kingdom is the phylum (plural: phyla). All vertebrates, for example, are classified into the phylum Chordata. Invertebrates are classified into many different phyla. All insects are placed in the phylum Uniramia, along with centipedes and millipedes. Spiders are in the phylum Chelicerata, with scorpions, pseudoscorpions, mites and ticks. Slaters are placed in the phylum Crustacea with crabs and yabbies. Snails and slugs are in the phylum Mollusca.

There are currently about 30 phyla in the animal world. These and other groupings are convenient in that they immediately give some indication of an animal's shape, habits, life history and evolutionary history.

WHAT IS A SPECIES?

A species is a kind (or type) of animal that cannot successfully breed with any type of animal other than its own kind. Human beings are all a single species and can therefore interbreed with their own kind. Different species look different from each other, although the differences can sometimes be very difficult to determine. They also generally live in different habitats to each other and have different ways of obtaining food. In other words, they have different ways of life.

An insect's common name may vary from State to State and even between regions within a State. Some insect species may have seven or eight common names. Many common names are also misleading, such as white ants (termites), Blue Ants (Diamma bicolor) and velvet ants (both wasps) and the Red Lacewing (a butterfly). Other names are borrowed from vertebrates, such as the Leopard, Australian Gull, Common Albatross and Australian Crow (all butterflies).

Left: Like prawns and crayfish, crabs are crustaceans. This ghost crab patrols sandy beaches at night.

Invertebrate groups

Conservation Watch
Unlike conservation of other animals, conservation of invertebrates can be a project in your own backyard. Insects need lots of native plants without insecticides or herbicides.

There are about 30 different animal phyla on Earth. About two-thirds of these groups live in the sea or freshwater, but they make up less than 2% of the estimated number of invertebrate species. The estimated total number of invertebrate species is more than 16 million (including undiscovered species). In contrast, the estimated total number of vertebrate species in the world is 51,400.

Common name	Scientific classification	Estimated number of species on Earth	Percentage of total
Marine groups			
Corals, sea jellies, sea anemones	Cnidaria	10 000	Less than 1%
Comb jellies	Ctenophora	500	Less than 1%
Arrow worms	Chaetognatha	100	Less than 1%
Peanut worms	Sipuncula	330	Less than 1%
Spoon worms	Echiura	140	Less than 1%
Beardworms	Pogonophora	500	Less than 1%
Lamp shells	Brachiopoda	500	Less than 1%
Starfish, urchins, sea cucumbers	Echinodermata	8 000	Less than 1%
Acorn worms	Hemichordata	150	Less than 1%
Phoronids	Phoronida	20	Less than 1%
Mostly marine groups			
Gnathostomulids	Gnathostomulida	1 000	Less than 1%
Molluscs	Mollusca	150 000	Less than 1%
Ribbon worms	Nemertinea	3 000	Less than 1%
Crabs, crayfish, slaters	Crustacea	150 000	Less than 1%
Bryozoans	Bryozoa	4 000	Less than 1%
Marine and freshwater groups			
Gastrotrichs	Gastrotricha	1 000	Less than 1%
Rotifers	Rotifera	3 000	Less than 1%
Kinorhynchs	Kinorhyncha	500	Less than 1%
Priapulids	Priapulida	25	Less than 1%
Water bears	Tardigrada	1 000	Less than 1%
Mostly terrestrial groups			
Velvetworms	Onychophora	300	Less than 1%
Insects, millipedes, centipedes	Arthropoda (sub-group Uniramia)	15 000 000	**93%**
Spiders, scorpions, mites	Arthropoda (sub-group Chelicerata)	160 000	Less than 1%
Mostly parasitic groups			
Mesozoans	Mesozoa	500	Less than 1%
Horsehair worms	Nematomorpha	275	Less than 1%
Flatworms, tapeworms	Platyhelminthes	50 000	Less than 1%
Thorny-headed worms	Acanthocephala	1 000	Less than 1%
Pentastomids	Pentastomida	100	Less than 1%
Groups found in all habitats			
Roundworms	Nematoda	500 000	**3%**
Earthworms, leeches	Annelida	25 000	Less than 1%
Vertebrates	Chordata	51 400	Less than 1%
Total		**16 122 340**	**100%**

MODIFIED FROM MEGLITSCH, P.A. & SCHRAM, F.R., 1991, *INVERTEBRATE ZOOLOGY*, THIRD EDITION, OXFORD UNIVERSITY PRESS, NEW YORK.
CHAPMAN, A.D., 2005, *NUMBERS OF LIVING SPECIES IN AUSTRALIA AND THE WORLD*, REPORT FOR THE DEPARTMENT OF ENVIRONMENT AND HERITAGE, AUSTRALIA.

the FACTS!

UNTIL RECENTLY, insects, spiders, crustaceans and other related groups were classified in the phylum Arthropoda (meaning "joint-legged"). However, arthropods have now been broken up into several different groups.

CHRISTMAS TREE WORMS (below) are common on the Great Barrier Reef in Queensland. When a shadow passes over them, they vanish in the blink of an eye.

MOST BIVALVE MOLLUSCS stay in one place, but some, like the file shell below, have rows of "tentacles" and can swim short distances by squirting out water.

Australia's amazing insects & spiders

Australia has a unique collection of insects and spiders, ranging from ancient species surviving here for the last 150 million years to recent accidental, deliberate or natural arrivals. Australia's long period of isolation from the rest of the world has enabled relatively ancient groups (such as bull ants and cave-dwelling spiders) to survive on the continent. These groups include some of the most fascinating insects and spiders currently on Earth.

THE FAUNA OF AUSTRALIA is not dominated by reptiles, birds or even mammals; it is dominated by invertebrates — particularly insects. Invertebrates are by far the most successful group of organisms that have ever existed on Earth and are a major influence on almost every terrestrial and freshwater environment.

Above: Cairns Birdwing Butterfly caterpillar.

Right, centre: Leaf beetles are small yet have a big impact on native ecosystems.

Far right, top: Shield bugs belong to the "true bugs" group.

Bottom, left: Bird-eating spider.

Bottom, right: Slater.

Presently, more insect species exist in Australia than all other animals and plants combined. On the average suburban block there are probably more insects and spiders than there are people in your State. Insects live in a huge range of habitats — on and in freshwater streams; on the intertidal zone of beaches; in soil and leaf litter; in living, dying and dead wood; and feeding on plant roots, leaves, flowers, seeds, fruits, pollen and nectar. They are found on and inside living animals, as well as in animal dung, dead animals and birds' nests. Insects colonise our houses and feed on our food, furniture, books, houses and even us; almost every possible environment is exploited by them.

the FACTS!

THE WORD "INSECT" comes from the Latin word *insectum*, which means "cut up" and refers to the way the insect body is divided into three distinct sections.

SPIDERS ARE ARACHNIDS and many early arachnids were very large. The 300-million-year-old scorpion *Brontoscorpio anglicus* was up to 80 cm long.

EARLY GIANTS

The first insects on Earth were wingless and very different from the beetles and butterflies seen today. They appeared on the edges of shallow lakes hundreds of millions of years before the first dinosaurs. The first spiders appeared more than 300 million years ago, living on the ground in the warm, moist forests of the Carboniferous Period. Early insect life was dominated by primitive groups such as cockroaches and silverfish that fed on rotting plant material. Later insects chewed leaves and sucked sap from living plants. Only with the evolution of flowers did pollinators and nectar-feeding insects appear.

Conservation Watch

A number of Governments and other authorities have set up rules about collecting and keeping insects. This is designed to prevent harm to natural insect populations.

INSECT FAMILY HISTORY

Era	Period	Millions of years ago	Appearance of each insect order
Cenozoic	Quaternary Present	1.8–present	Zorapterans (Zoraptera) Lice (Phthiraptera) Proturans (Protura)
Cenozoic	Tertiary	65–1.8	Mantids (Mantodea)
Mesozoic	Cretaceous	141–65	Termites (Isoptera) Fleas (Siphonaptera) Stylops (Strepsiptera)
Mesozoic	Jurassic	205–141	Earwigs (Dermaptera) Butterflies and moths (Lepidoptera)
Mesozoic	Triassic	250–205	Dragonflies (Odonata) Stick insects (Phasmatodea) Caddisflies (Trichoptera) Ants, bees and wasps (Hymenoptera)
Palaeozoic	Permian	298–250	Dobsonflies (Megaloptera) Scorpionflies (Mecoptera) Flies (Diptera) Stoneflies (Plecoptera) Webspinners (Embioptera) Beetles (Coleoptera) Booklice (Psocoptera) Thrips (Thysanoptera) Bugs (Hemiptera) Lacewings (Neuroptera)
Palaeozoic	Carboniferous	354–298	Diplurans (Diplura) Silverfish (Thysanura) Mayflies (Ephemeroptera) Grasshoppers (Orthoptera) Cockroaches (Blattodea)
Palaeozoic	Devonian	410–354	Bristletails (Archaeognatha) Springtails (Collembola)

MODIFIED FROM TIM NEW, 1992, *INTRODUCTORY ENTOMOLOGY FOR AUSTRALIAN STUDENTS*, NEW SOUTH WALES UNIVERSITY PRESS, SYDNEY

Top: Moth caterpillars may be protected by sharp spines.

Left: Many caterpillars have appendages on their bodies, which are possibly used to help sense their environment.

Below: With small bodies, cryptic colours and long legs, many spiders are well camouflaged and difficult to see.

the FACTS!

SEXTON BEETLES feed on dead animals. They work cooperatively and are able to strip and bury a dead mouse within a few minutes.

RHINOCEROS BEETLES are able to lift 850 times their own weight.

MAHOUT BEETLES sit on the heads of worker termites and ride around inside the termite nest. When two worker termites meet to exchange food, the beetle leans forward and takes some for itself.

THE NUMBER OF INSECTS in a swarm of Australian Plague Locusts (*Chortoicetes terminifera*) may be many times the number of people in Australia. These swarms can consume up to 100 tonnes of food each day. This is equal in weight to about 100 family cars.

BURYING BEETLES live in dead bodies in very unhealthy conditions, so adults produce secretions that have antibiotic qualities. These secretions kill any microorganisms on their bodies.

UNTIL A COUPLE OF HUNDRED years ago, most people believed insects arose by "spontaneous generation", being born out of the dew on leaves or even out of thin air.

ALTHOUGH INDIVIDUALLY TINY in comparison, the weight of all the ants on Earth is much greater than the weight of all humans on Earth.

THE SCUTTLE FLY (*Megaselia scalaris*) has successfully lived in emulsion paint, shoe polish, human bodies pickled in formalin and the lungs of living people.

SOME INSECTS USE TOOLS in their daily lives. Wasps and ants may use small stones to tamp down soil or block the holes of rival nests.

Introduction

Above: Each insect is designed for its particular way of life. With spike-laden forearms, praying mantids are designed to be lethal, efficient predators.

What makes an insect?

Adult insects have three distinct body parts. The head bears the antennae, mouth and compound eyes; the thorax carries three pairs of legs and usually two pairs of wings; and the abdomen contains many of the insect's body systems as well as its reproductive organs.

the FACTS!

THE COMPOUND EYES of male Orchard Butterflies are each made up of more than 18,000 simple eyes (each called an ommatidium).

THE WAY COMPOUND EYES (below) are constructed, means insects are usually very good at detecting movement and are able to flee when approached.

THE ANTENNAE of some male moths and beetles are elaborately branched like feathers (below), to pick up the slightest trace of a female's presence.

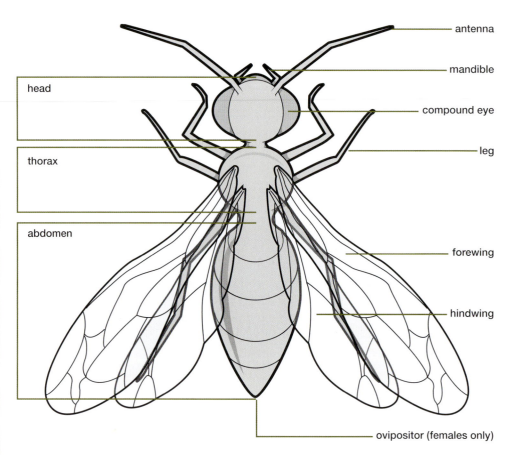

THE FRONT END

Most insects possess a pair of compound eyes on the head, made up of hundreds or thousands of simple eyes called ommatidia. This gives them a view of the world made up of many tiny dots, similar to the way we see a photo in a newspaper. An insect's antennae are used to detect chemicals in the environment, in much the same way that our noses are used for smell. Flying insects use antennae to detect air movement or wind speed.

THE MOUTHPARTS of insects are adapted to suit each particular feeding style and can be used to distinguish different insect groups. Beetles and grasshoppers, for example, have strong mandibles for chewing leaves, wood and other insects. Bugs have syringe-like mouthparts, as do mosquitoes, for piercing and sucking up plant sap and animal blood.

THE MIDDLE BIT

Most insects possess three pairs of legs, although juvenile insects such as maggots may have no legs at all and many caterpillars have added several pairs of false legs along the length of their bodies. Most adult insects carry two pairs of wings (forewings and hindwings), but flies have reduced them to one pair and fleas have lost them altogether. Groups such as earwigs and beetles have modified the forewings into protective coverings for the hindwings. Only adult insects have wings and, unlike legs, these cannot be repaired or replaced if damaged.

BRINGING UP THE REAR

The abdomen of insects is made up of eleven segments, which can be clearly seen in many species, but which may be reduced or less visible in others. Internally, the abdomen contains the bulk of the digestive system, as well as fat storage and the reproductive system. Abdomens of females are generally much larger than those of males, as females may have to carry many hundreds of eggs. Females may also possess a tube at the end of the abdomen for laying eggs. This tube is called an ovipositor, and it may also be modified into a sting.

Above: All insect abdomens are segmented, although the segments are not always as clearly visible as those of this stick insect.

Above, left: Leaf munchers like this katydid have medium-sized heads with small but strong chewing mouthparts.

Above: The compound eyes of cicadas are located on the sides of the head, while the three ocelli are in the centre.

Left: The insect's thorax supports the legs and wings. Wing buds can be seen on the thorax of this young stick insect.

the FACTS!

OCELLI are the three very simple eyes (top right), in the centre of the head. Most adult insects possess them, and no one is exactly sure what they do — although they possibly specialise in detecting light and dark.

SOME AQUATIC INSECTS have legs modified into oars for rowing, whereas grasshoppers have powerful legs that enable them to jump long distances.

INSTEAD OF COMPOUND EYES, juvenile insects such as caterpillars have between one and six eyes, called stemmata, on each side of the head. The stemmata can probably detect light and dark, as well as basic shapes.

THE MOUTHPARTS of a butterfly or moth are modified into a long tube used for drinking nectar. This tube is coiled up under the head when not in use. Some moths have no mouthparts whatsoever and do not feed as adults.

THE INSECT EXOSKELETON is made from tough layers of protein and other compounds. The wing of this tree cricket (below) has holes to let air through.

Lepidoptera

Above: Caper White Butterflies undergo massive migrations in years when strong winds blow consistently in the same direction.

Right: Monarch Butterflies are also known as Wanderers. Adults reached Australia more than 100 years ago by "wandering" across the ocean.

Butterflies
— flying jewels

Class: Insecta
Order: Lepidoptera

No group of insects gives us more pleasure than the butterflies. Although one of the smaller groups of insects in terms of species numbers, they are certainly the best studied group but there are still butterfly species in Australia that remain undiscovered. Some butterflies are even being threatened with extinction by habitat destruction and other human activities.

the FACTS!

ALTHOUGH they look fearsome, the spines on the Common Eggfly caterpillar (below) are harmless.

MANY PEOPLE think butterflies only live for one day. In fact, some butterflies live for many months and undergo a dormant period when they will sit motionless for weeks on end during unfavourable times.

CATERPILLARS of the Common Imperial Blue butterfly (*Jalmenus evagoras*) can produce a clicking sound. This is probably to communicate with the ants that look after them.

MALE BUTTERFLIES may be territorial, chasing other butterflies and even birds and humans away from their chosen patch of ground.

FEMALES of some butterfly species may lay more than 2000 eggs each. Of these, only two generally make it all the way to adulthood and reproduce themselves.

KEY PLAYERS

Butterflies are perhaps the best known insects and are important for their role as pollinators and the general role both adults and caterpillars play in Australian ecosystems. Although caterpillars can sometimes be damaging to plants, their chewing usefully recycles nutrients from plants back into the soil and they are also an important food source for birds and other animals.

Butterflies are particularly abundant in tropical areas and least common in desert areas where water is scarce. Almost three quarters of Australian species are found in northern Queensland.

Tropical butterflies, such as the Ulysses Butterfly (*Papilio ulysses*) and the Cairns Birdwing Butterfly (*Ornithoptera priamus*), also tend to be larger and more colourful than species living further south. Some smaller butterflies, such as the Southern Sedge-darter (*Telicota eurychlora*), live in very specific habitats, such as swampland at the edge of rivers, restricted by the distribution of the caterpillars' food plants.

COLOURS FOR SURVIVAL

The colours and patterns of butterfly wings, although highly appealing, are not there for our benefit. Each butterfly must survive and reproduce against the odds and the wings are designed to assist with survival. The wings of some species, such as the male Cruiser Butterfly (*Vindula arsinoe*, below), imitate dead leaves and the butterfly is almost invisible as it sits among leaf litter.

Conservation Watch

A survey of endangered butterflies in Switzerland found ten separate threats to their survival. The greatest threat is the impact of agriculture.

Above: The Blue-banded Eggfly (*Hypolimnas alimena*) is one of a number of species of butterflies called eggflies.

THE STRIPES on the wings of the Lurcher Butterfly (*Yoma sabina*) help break up its outline when it is basking in the sun. The orange and black pattern of butterflies such as the Wanderer Butterfly (*Danaus plexippus*), or Orange Lacewing (*Cethosia penthesilea*) alert predators that the butterflies are distasteful or poisonous. In general, butterflies with very bright colours on top of the wings, used to attract mates, have undersides that are very dull, so that the butterfly all but disappears when the wings are closed. The Ulysses Butterfly (*Papilio ulysses*) is an excellent example of this.

A LIFE IN FOUR STAGES

There are four stages in the butterfly life cycle — egg, caterpillar, pupa (or chrysalis) and adult. Caterpillars eat constantly, growing rapidly and obtaining all the nutrients needed for later in life. Most caterpillars eat leaves, but some species feed on flowers or seeds and a few live in ant nests feeding on the larvae within. The pupa is a resting stage in which, remarkably, the caterpillar's tissues are broken down and an adult is built in its place. Although both caterpillars and adult butterflies are able to defend themselves to some extent, the pupae cannot. They are, therefore, hidden away from the food plant, or so well camouflaged in shape and colour that they are almost invisible on the plant. Adult butterflies can only drink liquids and feed on nectar, but some species will drink from puddles or from the fermenting juices of rotting fruit or dead animals.

Above: Scales on the upper wings of the Ulysses Butterfly refract light to give the wings their beautiful blue.

Above: Skippers are a family of small, fast-flying butterflies. They are mostly coloured brown, orange or yellow.

A JEWELLED GARDEN

In Australia, butterflies have been disappearing from habitats for many years, particularly as humans expand into bushland with housing developments. The main problem is a reduction in suitable food plants for the caterpillars; adult butterflies can feed from a great range of flowering plants, but the caterpillars can only feed on the leaves of certain plant species. While a few caterpillars, such as those of the Cabbage White Butterfly (*Pieris rapae*), will feed on more than 150 different food plants, many butterflies are restricted to only two or three plant species. In recent years, butterflies are starting to come back to suburban areas as gardeners plant more and more suitable plant species. It is easy to develop a butterfly garden and there are plenty of books and websites on the topic.

the FACTS!

THE LARGEST BUTTERFLY in the world is the endangered Queen Alexandra Birdwing (*Ornithoptera alexandrae*) of New Guinea. The first collected specimen was brought down with a shotgun.

WITH A WINGSPAN of up to 180 mm, the female of the Cairns Birdwing Butterfly (*Ornithoptera priamus*, (top right) is the largest butterfly in Australia.

SOME BUTTERFLIES are highly adaptable. The Lesser Wanderer (*Danaus chrysippus*) takes 23 days to develop from egg to adult in the warmer parts of its range, but almost a year in colder areas.

WANDERER BUTTERFLIES (*Danaus plexippus*) undergo a migration in North America of more than 3000 km each year, travelling higher than 100 m off the ground at speeds of up to 40 km/h and losing about one third of their body weight.

BUTTERFLIES CAN FLY long distances. In some years, the Common Eggfly (*Hypolimnas bolina*, below) flies all the way across the sea from Australia to New Zealand.

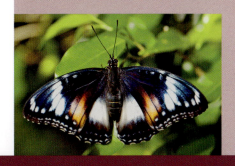

Lepidoptera

Above: Although most moths sit with their wings flat, some species fold the wings above and around the body when at rest.

Top, right: Some moths, particularly nocturnal species, display eye spots that may resemble the eyes of owls.

Moths
— night flyers

Class: Insecta
Order: Lepidoptera

Moths are closely related to butterflies and are part of the same group, the order Lepidoptera. There are, however, many more types of moths in Australia than butterflies. Moths can be distinguished from butterflies by several physical and behavioural features but, as always, there are exceptions to each feature.

the FACTS!

THE TONGUE (haustellum) of the Madagascar Hawk Moth may be 300 mm long.

THE MOTH WITH THE LARGEST wingspan in Australia is the Hercules Moth (*Coscinocera hercules*). It measures 270 mm across and has the largest wing area of any moth in the world. The caterpillars grow up to 120 mm and can weigh 29 g.

COCOONS SPUN by moth caterpillars can be extremely tough. Some cocoons are so strong and fibrous they cannot be cut with a pair of scissors.

THE CATERPILLARS of butterflies are usually smooth and often hairless. Moth caterpillars may be covered with long hairs, bristles (scoli) or poisonous spines.

MOTHS VS BUTTERFLIES

The four main differences between moths and butterflies are:

- Moths fly at night. Butterflies fly during the day.
- Moths are generally not as colourful.
- Moths sit with their wings flat. Butterflies hold their wings above their bodies.
- Moths have feathery antennae. Butterflies have "clubbed" antennae.

EXCEPTIONAL MOTHS

However, there are some moths that fly during the day, particularly at dawn and dusk. Some of these moths are as colourful as the brightest butterflies, with blues, yellows and reds dominating. Not only do some moths sit with the wings above the body, but many butterflies sit with their wings held out to the side. To complicate matters further, a number of moth species have no wings at all, including female case moths, which never emerge from their cocoons. Many moths also have no mouthparts and do not feed as adults, living on the fat they stored as a caterpillar.

FEMALE MOTHS like this wingless Painted Apple Moth (*Teia anartoides*, left) lay eggs after mating, but some species produce fertile eggs without mating. Most species produce a couple of hundred eggs laid on or near a food plant. Others drop thousands of eggs randomly in flight.

Above: Caterpillars are basically eating machines. They may increase their size by many thousands of times from egg to pupa.

Bottom, right: Many moths have intricate wing patterns that can vary between individuals.

EATING MACHINES

Moth caterpillars are voracious eaters, consuming the leaves, branches, roots, wood, bark, flowers, fruit and seeds of food plants. There are probably no greater consumers of plants on Earth than moth caterpillars. Different species may consume the same part of the plant in different ways, such as caterpillars that burrow into the inside of leaves (leaf miners), those that scrape off only the top layer (skeletonisers) and others that consume the leaf entirely (leaf chewers).

Above: Although butterflies tend to be more colourful than moths, some moth species are as brightly coloured as the best of the butterflies.

Above: Not all moth wings are wide and flat. It is difficult to believe the wings of plume moths are able to get them off the ground.

URINE, BLOOD & ROTTING FRUIT

Like butterflies, adult moths feed through a long proboscis (haustellum). They can only feed on liquids, mostly nectar and water, but also mammal urine, sweat and tears, as well as liquids from rotting fruit and animal droppings. A few overseas species use their proboscis to pierce the skin of mammals to drink the blood. Several primitive moth species with reduced mouthparts are able to eat pollen and many species do not feed at all.

Right: The proboscis of this Hawk Moth helps it reach nectar in the base of flowers.

BECAUSE THERE ARE SO MANY MOTH SPECIES and because their caterpillars are such relentless consumers of plants, a number of species have become serious pests of crops around the world. Although the number of pest species is small compared to the total number of moth species, a few are able to cause serious damage to some stored grains (such as wheat and flour), fruit orchards, pastures and ornamental plants in gardens. On the other hand, moths such as Silkworms (*Bombyx mori*) have produced silk used by humans for at least five thousand years and many moth caterpillars have been successfully employed to control weeds that were accidentally introduced to Australia.

Left: Some moths have long legs and long, V-shaped wings. These moths are designed for speed.

the FACTS!

MANY MOTHS are able to hover like hummingbirds when drinking nectar from flowers. The Bee Moth (*Cephonodes kingii*) has clear wings and hovers like a giant bee when it is feeding.

NIGHT-FLYING tiger moths (below) are poisonous and bats have learnt not to eat them. When moths hear echolocating clicks from bats, they signal back and the bats veer away.

THE LIGHT BROWN Apple Moth (*Epiphyas postvittana*) is a pest of apples and other fruit in Australia. It has been accidentally exported to a number of countries where it is an even more serious pest.

CUP MOTH caterpillars (*Doratifera* spp.) have rosettes of stinging hairs on their backs. These hairs are hollow and are filled with a chemical called histamine, which can cause painful welts.

LOOPER CATERPILLARS belong to the family Geometridae, which means "earth measurers". They are also called "inch-worms", due to their habit of looping or "inching" the body forward as they move.

HAWK MOTHS are accomplished fliers and their bodies are built for speed. They have narrow pointed forewings and a long tapering body to reduce drag.

Ants
— activity unlimited

Above: Green Tree Ants form living chains to draw leaves close enough to be sewn together using silk from the larvae.

Right: Bull ants are both the largest and most primitive ants in the world.

Class: Insecta
Order: Hymenoptera

Ants have possibly the broadest diet of any group of insects. Larvae live in the nest building up their bodies, so they require lots of protein. Adult workers need energy to forage outside the nest, so consume mostly carbohydrates (sugars). Most ant species need a mix of foods from a range of sources, but some have developed specialist diets.

the FACTS!

QUEEN ANTS are long lived and may lay several million eggs over more than ten years.

ANTS MAY BE ONE OF THE earliest examples of biological pest control by humans. Green Tree Ants were used by Chinese farmers several hundred years ago to control pests in orchards.

AUSTRALIAN ANT SPECIES are highly diverse, even in desert regions. They will often live together successfully, with up to 150 different species coexisting within an area of less than 1 ha.

SPECIAL CHAMBERS within ant nests are kept aside as "nurseries" — places where the larvae are cared for (below).

MORE THAN 200 SPECIES of insect are known to live inside ant nests. They are called "inquilines" and some species will feed on the workers or larvae within the nest.

MALE ANTS HAVE WINGS throughout adult life, but queens shed or chew off their wings once they have mated.

MANY SPECIES, such as harvester ants, collect and horde vast quantities of seed within their nests to get them through lean times. Sugar ants (above), as their name suggests, are very attracted to sugar and will "farm" groups of aphids on plants for the sweet honeydew they produce. Other ants are specialist predators, feeding only on other ant species, or on termites, centipedes or slaters.

NESTING BY NUMBERS

The number of ants in a colony will depend on the species. Bull ants (*Myrmecia* spp.) may have fewer than 200 workers in a full-sized colony, whereas Green Tree Ant (*Oecophylla smaragdina*) colonies may hold many thousands of workers in dozens of separate nests covering several hectares. Most ants nest underground and search for food only at ground level.

SHARING HABITAT

Many different ant species are able to share the same habitat by dividing it up among them. Some species may forage in the trees while others never leave the ground, so the two never meet. A number of ant species forage only at night, whereas others venture out only in the early morning and still others wait until the middle of the day. The main way to live happily and avoid interactions is to divide up the food resources. Where one species feeds on seeds and another feeds only on insect eggs, the two species are never in competition with each other.

Below: Bull ants removing a dead worker from within the nest. Some ant species keep "rubbish tips" close to the entrance.

Bees
— nectar gatherers

Class: Insecta
Order: Hymenoptera

The best known bee in Australia is the European Honey Bee (Apis mellifera), which was introduced in 1822 and has now established itself over large areas of the continent. Many people think it is the only type of bee in Australia, but in fact there are nearly 2000 species of native bee. Some native Australian bees also make honey, but their honey is not as sweet and is produced only in relatively small quantities.

BEES GENERALLY FEED on nectar, which is full of sugars for energy, but they also eat pollen to obtain the protein needed for growth. Honey is made mostly from nectar and is the bees' way of storing food for lean times (such as winter) when fresh nectar and pollen may be unavailable.

Left: A Bumble Bee feeding. These were introduced into Tasmania in the 1990s and quickly spread throughout the State.

SMALL, DARK & STINGLESS

One of the most common native bees is the stingless Trigona (*Trigona* spp.). Trigona are small, dark bees that live in hollow branches or rock crevices, in colonies of thousands of workers. They build honeycomb made from resin from trees and wax from their own bodies, but the combs sit horizontally rather than hanging vertically like those of European Honey Bees. Cells in the comb house the bee larvae and larger wax pots are used to store honey and pollen. Trigona cannot sting, but defend the nest by crawling over and biting intruders.

BLUE TEDDIES

Most species of native bee are solitary. A single female will construct a burrow with a number of chambers in soil or wood, then provision each chamber with honey and pollen before laying an egg in each, sealing up the chambers, and flying away. After hatching, each bee larva feeds within its chamber until it is mature.

A type of bee commonly seen feeding at flowers is the Teddy Bear Bee or Blue Banded Bee (*Amegilla* sp.), named after the hairy brown thorax and blue-striped abdomen. They burrow into earthen banks and will return to the same place year after year, generating masses of nests. These and other bees show promise for use as pollinators for crops grown in glasshouses.

Conservation Watch
European Honey Bees (*Apis mellifera*, above) were introduced into Australia in 1822. There is some evidence that their activities can be harmful to the lives of native bees.

the FACTS!

EUROPEAN HONEY BEES are the only species other than humans that use a language comprised of symbols.

CUCKOO BEES do not make their own nests but lay eggs in other bees' nests when the owners are out foraging. When the owners return, they look after the cuckoo bee larvae as if they were their own.

BEES' COMMON NAMES may be derived from their activities. For example, carpenter bees (below) tunnel into wood and mason bees make burrows in bricks and mortar.

EUROPEAN HONEY BEES must make nearly 22 million trips to collect enough nectar to produce 1 kg of honey.

BEES PROBABLY evolved from a wasp-like ancestor that began to provision its nest with nectar and pollen instead of insect prey.

SOME BEES, including the European Honey Bee are able to remember the location of flowers after two months of winter hibernation. For insects, this is an exceptionally long memory.

Wasps
— diverse hunters

Class: Insecta
Order: Hymenoptera

Wasps are a remarkably diverse group of insects and include a subgroup called sawflies, named after the saw-like ovipositor of adult females. The female uses her saw to scrape off the outer layer of a leaf before inserting her eggs. Because they lack the pointed ovipositor of other wasps, sawflies are unable to sting. Sawflies are considered a primitive group of wasps, distinguished from other wasps by the lack of a narrow "waist" between the abdomen and thorax.

Above: Some wasps have a "furry" thorax, which demonstrates their relationship to bees.

Below, right: A male ichneumon wasp is attracted to a slipper orchid flower because its scent resembles that of a female wasp. The wasp carries pollen from the previous flower it visited.

WASPS ON WASPS

Most wasps live as parasites on other insects, including other wasps. One of the largest groups of parasitic wasps is the ichneumons, with more than 1200 species in Australia. Adults feed on flowers and are great pollinators of plants, while larvae parasitise and control pest insects. Ichneumons parasitise many different types of insects and spiders, using their ovipositors to bore into almost any location their hosts can hide in. Some large ichneumons that parasitise wood-boring insects may have ovipositors many times the length of their bodies.

the FACTS!

WASPS ARE one of the largest groups of insects in Australia, with more than 10,000 species recorded.

MANY PARASITIC wasps will lay their eggs randomly on leaves. The egg hatches when the leaf and egg are together eaten by a host caterpillar.

A TYPE OF SAWFLY, called the Pear and Cherry Slug, is an accidentally introduced pest of fruit trees. The male of this species has never been recorded in Australia.

FEMALE WINGLESS wasps are often confused with ants. "Velvet ants" (below) and "Blue Ants" (*Diamma bicolor*) are two examples.

SINGLE MUMS

Many wasps, including most sawflies, can reproduce without the need for males. This is known as "parthenogenesis". In fact, males of some species have never been discovered. Some species can produce only females by parthenogenesis, others can produce both males and females, but social wasps tend to produce females (or workers) from fertilised eggs and males from unfertilised eggs. These strategies enable females to determine the sex of their offspring (which may change with the season), or to reproduce rapidly without wasting time searching for a mate.

Conservation Watch

Only one species of wasp is listed as being of conservation concern in Australia. This is the Relict Braconid (*Parephedrus relictus*) in New South Wales. No species are protected by law in any State.

Above: A female paper wasp on her nest. She will readily defend the nest with her painful sting.

Below: Unlike most wasp species, sawflies lay their eggs on leaves and guard them until the eggs hatch.

PRIMITIVE REGURGITATORS

Unlike most wasp larvae, which are maggot-like and legless, sawfly larvae are more like the caterpillars of butterflies and moths. They have three pairs of legs and most species actively feed on leaves. The best known species in Australia is the Steelblue Sawfly (*Perga dorsalis*), whose larvae are commonly seen in large groups on gum trees (above left) during winter and are often known as "spitfires". Although harmless, spitfires store eucalyptus oils in their foreguts and, when disturbed, regurgitate large green blobs of oil from their mouths to deter predators.

Left: Wasps are commonly orange and black or orange and brown.

A GREAT DIVERSITY

The females of many wasp species, particularly those known as flower wasps, are wingless. Larvae of these species tend to live underground, parasitising mole crickets and beetle and bee larvae. When mature, the wingless female climbs to the top of a nearby plant and releases pheromones to attract a winged male.

Other wasps are social, forming massive colonies of thousands of workers, which may be numerous enough to influence the ecology of surrounding areas. In Australia, paper wasps are particularly common in the north, cooperatively building large exposed nests of wood fibre mixed with their saliva. Unfortunately the European Wasp (*Vespula germanica*), an aggressive introduced member of this group, is probably the best known wasp in Australia.

Another well known group is the mud wasps. The female builds a small nest of mud or clay mixed with saliva and provisions it with a number of caterpillars or spiders, paralysed by her sting. She lays a single egg in the nest before sealing it up, leaving her offspring to its own devices. After hatching, the larva feeds on the paralysed hosts before pupating and emerging from the nest to continue the cycle.

Less well-known are the gall-forming wasps. These species tend to be very small and lay their eggs in plant tissue. The wasp larva feeds inside the stems and leaves of plants, forming a large, obvious outgrowth called a "gall". The plant itself forms the gall in response to chemicals released by the wasp larva. Many gall-forming wasps are sought out and parasitised by other wasp species.

the FACTS!

GROUPS OF SAWFLIES generally follow a particular leader when feeding and a single individual will tap the tip of its abdomen on a branch to communicate with the rest of the group if it becomes separated.

CUCKOO WASPS (below) lay their eggs in the mud nests of other wasps, usually before the nest is completed. The cuckoo wasp larva feeds on the paralysed prey supplied by the nest's builder.

DURING MATING, male flower wasps may feed regurgitated honeydew to the female. The honeydew is collected from sap-feeding leaf hoppers.

MANY PARASITIC WASPS are sold commercially to control insect pests in greenhouses.

Coleoptera

Above: Ladybirds come in a range of colours.

Below: Longicorn beetle.

Beetles
— beetle mania

Class: Insecta
Order: Coleoptera

Beetles are the largest group of animals on Earth. About one third of all animal species are beetles. They are found all over Australia in every possible habitat on land and in fresh water. In just one beetle family alone, the weevils, there are several thousand different species — this is as many as all the dragonflies, cockroaches, mantids, grasshoppers, termites, stick insects, earwigs and lacewings combined.

IT'S ALL IN THE WINGS

Beetles can be distinguished from other groups of insects by their hardened forewings. This gives them their order name Coleoptera, which means "sheath wings". Beetles lift their forewings up during flight and use only their transparent hindwings to fly. In some species, particularly weevils, the forewings are fused together, making the species flightless. Other species, such as rove beetles, have very short forewings, so the hindwings can be seen folded beneath them at rest. Occasionally, in groups such as fireflies, the males are winged and the females wingless.

the FACTS!

SOME BEETLE FAMILIES live in ponds and streams and have evolved gills to help them breathe under water.

SOME LEAF BEETLES and ground beetles give birth to live young. The eggs are stored in the female's reproductive tube until after they hatch.

IN SOME BIZARRE beetle species, such as micromalthid beetles, there is no pupal stage for females. They are able to reproduce while still indistinguishable from the larval stage.

SPANISH DUNG BEETLES have been imported into some parts of Australia to try to reduce the number of dog droppings in suburban parks.

ALTHOUGH BEETLES all share the same simple body plan, they live in just about every type of environment and engage in every imaginable way of life. Beetle larvae can be distinguished from other types of insect larvae by the hardened head capsule with strong, chewing mouthparts. They generally feed on living plants or rotting wood, but many species are predatory, parasitic, or feed on dung or dead animals. The tiny larvae of rhipiphorid beetles hatch from eggs laid in flower heads, then attach themselves to visiting bees or wasps. The larva is taken back to the nest where it feeds on the bee or wasp larvae. The wide range of larval adaptations is one of the reasons there are so many beetle species. Some jewel beetles will spend several decades feeding as larvae, emerging as adults that do not feed at all and live only a couple of weeks.

Left: Passalid beetles live in communal groups under logs. The adults feed the larvae chewed wood until they pupate.

Right: Many beetle grubs look similar but differences can be easily distinguished at family level.

Male beetles often have larger antennae than females, used for picking up the smells (or "pheromones") of nearby females. A number of beetles are known to produce quite powerful pheromones that can be detected over long distances, as well as other pheromones designed to form gatherings of males and females for mating. Male rhinoceros and stag beetles are armed with greatly enlarged horns or mandibles for battling other males; victors are more likely to mate with available females. Parental care is well known among beetle groups. Some water beetle species carry the eggs around on the abdomen until they hatch, while several species of ground beetles store seeds as food for the larvae. Dung beetles are well known for digging special chambers in the ground and adding animal dung to feed their larvae. Burying beetles do the same with scraps from animal carcasses.

Coleoptera

UNIQUELY AUSSIE

Australian beetles as a group are different to beetles in other parts of the world. There are many beetle species or even families and subfamilies that are found nowhere else. The make-up of Australia's beetles reflects their long evolutionary history and includes influences from elsewhere as different groups have made their way to Australia over millions of years. The long relationship between beetles and their host plants, particularly gum trees and wattles, means that families such as leaf beetles are well represented. One of the reasons Australia is home to so many species of gum tree is that they are constantly under attack from hundreds of leaf beetle species. The gum trees are continuously changing, or forming new species, to try and avoid the hungry leaf beetle larvae.

Above: Christmas beetles are some of the best known beetles in Australia. They are so named because they are most common around Christmas.

Above, left to right: Most weevils are characterised by a long snout, or rostrum. The mouthparts are located at the tip of the snout; Tortoise beetles have flattened transparent edges that can be pressed against the surface of a leaf to protect their undersides; Scarabs are probably the best known beetles in the world and are also one of the largest families; Belid beetles are closely related to weevils, as demonstrated by the long proboscis.

the FACTS!

THE LARGEST BEETLE in Australia is Wallace's Longicorn (*Batocera wallacei*) from the tip of Cape York Peninsula. It has a body length of 85 mm and its antennae may span 400 mm.

THE SMALLEST BEETLE in the world is the Feather-winged Beetle (*Nanosella fungi*), which is smaller than a full stop on this page.

SOME BEETLE LARVAE possess a special spine called an "egg burster", used to help break through the egg shell during hatching.

THERE ARE MORE than 110 different families of beetle recorded from Australia.

SOME BEETLES, such as ladybirds, may defend themselves using "reflex bleeding". When threatened, the beetle oozes blood, which may be toxic to predators, from joints in its body.

Above: Jewel beetles include some of the most spectacular and colourful beetles in the world.

Right: Stag Beetle males have enlarged mandibles that can be used to fight other males for the right to mate.

Flies
— two-winged acrobats

Above: Many types of blowfly feed on animal wastes. Fresh droppings will cause a feeding frenzy among a number of different fly species.

Class: Insecta
Order: Diptera

All Australians are familiar with flies and the problems they sometimes cause during summer. There are only a few fly species that bother humans; the vast majority of flies never come near us and are important components of natural ecosystems. Many flies are essential pollinators of plants and the maggots of some species are even important in controlling weeds. A great number are predators or parasites of other insects. Without maggots, which help remove decomposing bodies, the ground would be littered with rotting animal carcasses.

the FACTS!

THE TASTE BUDS on the feet of flies are 10 million times more sensitive than those on the human tongue.

THE LARGEST FLY in Australia is the Giant Robber Fly (*Phellus olgae*), with a wingspan of 80 mm. It occurs across southern and eastern Australia.

THE REPRODUCTIVE abilities of house flies are enormous. The descendants of a single pair, provided that all survived, would reach 190 quintillion flies (190,000,000,000,000,000,000) within five months.

CRANEFLIES (below) are the largest fly family in Australia, with more than 700 species. They have thin bodies and very long legs, and many are striped orange and black.

LIKE A NUMBER OF OTHER insects, flies have taste buds in their feet, as well as other places around the body (such as the mouthparts and antennae).

SOME SPECIES of flesh fly are parasitic. In an example of turning the tables, one species parasitises the Sydney Funnelweb Spider (*Atrax robustus*).

THE FLIES THAT BITE

In Australia, Bush Flies (*Musca vetustissima*) are sometimes said to bite but in fact they have no teeth. They may be able to rasp the sensitive skin around people's eyes in order to encourage secretions such as tears, but they are unable to actually bite. Bush Flies also feed on our saliva, mucus, blood and faeces for protein, water and minerals. Protein is required by females to produce eggs, but otherwise they live on sugar and water. They can live for about one week in warm weather and for two to four weeks in cool weather, but only survive about one day without water.

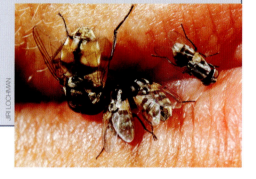

MIDGES OR BLACKFLIES are able to bite humans and, in some coastal areas of Australia, very large numbers of tiny biting midges can cause lesions and welts to humans, which can be extremely itchy. In other parts of the world, such as the USA, aquatic biting midges and blackflies are so abundant that creeks and other waterways are out of bounds to people at certain times of the year.

Above: Not all flies have wings. These wingless species are nicknamed "walks".

Right: As its name suggests, the Giant Mosquito is one of the largest in Australia. It does not cause problems to humans.

THE DREADED AUSSIE MOZZIE

Both male and female mosquitoes feed on nectar from flowers to satisfy their own food requirements, but females also need protein to produce enough eggs. Human and animal blood has plenty of protein, so mosquitoes extract this blood from us and other animals to make eggs. Several blood meals are usually required before the eggs can be formed. Unfortunately, by extracting our blood the mosquito often leaves behind chemicals that cause us to itch and may also pass on a number of diseases (such as dengue fever).

Dragonflies & damselflies
— wolves on the wing

Class: Insecta
Order: Odonata

Dragonflies and damselflies are two related groups, together making up the order Odonata. Both groups are active predators with aquatic nymphs; adults are commonly seen around Australia's waterways.

THE BEHAVIOUR of dragonflies puts most species into one of two categories — "perchers", which spend most of their time perching on vegetation and make short flights to catch passing prey, or "hawkers", which patrol continually, chasing down any flying insect unlucky enough to stray within sight. Many dragonfly and damselfly species are also extremely territorial — the males in particular will fight off any intruder that ventures into their patch.

Above: This species is found across northern Australia, as well as New Guinea and New Caledonia.

Below: The underside of a dragonfly nymph. The prominent "mask" can be seen underneath the head.

Top: The Baron Dragonfly (*Hemianax papuensis*) is common in southern and eastern Australia, particularly during the height of summer.

Above: The large compound eyes can be seen on this dragonfly as it rests on an aquatic reed.

MASKED PREDATORS

Dragonfly and damselfly nymphs (juveniles) are almost exclusively aquatic. Two sets of large hooks, located on the "mask" beneath the head, can be extended outwards to grasp passing invertebrates. After hatching, nymphs eat tiny crustaceans, progressing to aquatic beetles, snails, water bugs and fish as they grow.

the FACTS!

SOME DRAGONFLIES can fly at more than 50 km/h in short bursts.

THE DRAGONFLY *Petalura ingentissima* from the tip of Cape York Peninsula has a wingspan of 165 mm and is the largest dragonfly species in Australia.

FEMALE DRAGONFLIES may drop their eggs onto wet roads, mistaking the reflection of the road for that of a creek or pond.

DRAGONFLIES TEND to be much larger and more robust than damselflies and perch with their wings held out to the sides. While resting, damselflies hold their wings behind them.

THE LEGS OF DRAGONFLIES are held in a basket-like arrangement designed for catching flying prey (below). They have difficulty walking, as the legs are uneven and can only bend forwards.

THE WHEEL DEAL

Dragonflies and damselflies mate in the "wheel position", unique among insects. The male grasps the female's head or thorax with special claspers at the tip of his abdomen, while the female bends the tip of her abdomen up to meet the front of his. In this position, sperm is transferred from the male to the female while both partners are still able to fly around. After mating, the female typically lays eggs in the water or inserts them into aquatic plants just under or above the water surface. The male often remains attached to the female during egg-laying or hovers close by, guarding her from any other interested males.

Left: Damselflies mating.

Mantids
— perfect predators

Class: Insecta
Order: Mantodea

Above: The jaws of a large mantid are very powerful but delicate enough to gently clean the tips of its legs.

Right: The common Green Mantid has a blue eye-spot on each foreleg; these eyespots are used to startle predators.

Mantids are superb insect predators, perfectly adapted to their hunting way of life. They have large eyes on a head that can move freely in any direction, giving them a wide field of vision. A mantid's thorax is long and movable, while its legs are long and slender. These features together enable the mantid to reach forward over a greater distance. Most importantly, the forelegs are highly modified with rows of large spines and are held against the body in a typical "praying" position before striking at passing prey.

the FACTS!

IN SOME MANTID SPECIES the female mantid guards the ootheca (egg package) until the eggs hatch, but in most species females move away soon after egg-laying.

TINY PARASITIC WASPS may lay their eggs in mantid oothecae. The wasp larvae consume the mantid eggs and then emerge as adult wasps. Some oothecae end up producing more wasps than mantids.

MANTID JAWS (below) are extremely strong. The largest Australian species can draw blood if allowed to bite a person's hand. When approached, however, mantids will generally try to hide.

PUNCHING ABOVE THEIR WEIGHT

Australia's tropical mantids (*Hierodula* spp.) are some of the largest in the world. These mantids have been recorded capturing and eating Green Tree-frogs (*Litoria caerulea*) more than three times their own weight, as well as small birds such as honeyeaters. Mantids are almost always ambush predators, waiting for prey to come within range rather than actively hunting it down. Their skill as predators is demonstrated by their ability to capture the largest dragonflies. Because mantids are predatory at all stages of their lives, they live a solitary existence and come together only for mating.

Most mantids may be found hunting among foliage, but different species may live on tree trunks or even on the ground. Both sexes are generally winged and the female is usually larger than the male. However, in some species the female may be wingless or have very short wings and be unable to fly.

LOVE AT FIRST BITE

The adult female may eat the male during or after mating (and even eat his head before). This provides much needed protein for egg production. The female then produces up to 400 eggs inside a protective ootheca. The ootheca is made from a foamy material produced from the female's abdomen, which she moulds with her legs into a tough capsule. Oothecae can be found on branches, fences and clothes lines.

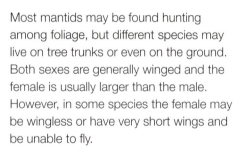

PROBABLY THE BEST KNOWN mantid in Australia is the Green Mantid (*Orthodera ministralis*). This species grows up to 50 mm long and is common in gardens during summer.

*Above: The leaf-like Netwinged Mantid (*Neomantis australis*) is found in tropical Australian rainforests.*

Right: A wingless female amorphoscelid mantid. This species lives on the ground and may feed on ants.

Stick insects
— masters of disguise

Class: Insecta
Order: Phasmatodea

Stick insects, as the name suggests, are generally long and thin with bodies resembling small twigs or sticks. Their legs are not adapted for jumping, digging or holding prey, but for clinging to branches in the wind. All species are plant feeders and most are tropical. A few southern species that feed on gum trees will sometimes increase their population to enormous numbers, defoliating whole areas of forest.

Above: Peppermint Stick Insect.

the FACTS!

THE TITAN STICK INSECT (*Acrophylla titan*), which grows up to 260 mm long, is one of the longest in Australia, while the Goliath Stick Insect (*Eurycnema goliath*), weighing up to 30 g, is the heaviest.

SEVERAL STICK INSECT species that are normally solitary may change colour when their populations build up to high densities, moving from plain green to yellow and black. This may help them avoid predators.

ONE FAMILY of stick insects, called leaf insects, have greatly flattened bodies that give them a remarkable resemblance to leaves. Leaf insects occur in Tropical North Queensland.

STICK INSECTS are commonly kept as pets around the world. The most valuable species are sometimes traded for high prices.

SOME STICK INSECTS stop moving and drop to the ground when disturbed. Their camouflage makes them very difficult to find among the leaf litter.

STARTLING DECEIVERS

Stick insects generally rely on camouflage to protect themselves from predators. However, some species also have "startle displays" that are used when camouflage fails. Goliath Stick Insects (*Eurycnema goliath*, above left) have bright crimson hindwings that are suddenly exposed when the insect is disturbed. Peppermint Stick Insects (*Megacrania batesii*) squirt predators with an accurate stream of white, minty-smelling liquid that causes a burning sensation to sensitive membranes such as eyes. Other stick insects loudly and rapidly rustle their hindwings when disturbed.

A CHOICE OF OFFSPRING

Stick insects tend to be slow-moving, solitary insects, rarely coming together except to mate. The female of many stick insect species is wingless or too heavy to fly even if she does have wings. In most species, the male possesses wings but is a poor flier. Many female stick insects are able to reproduce without mating and, in some species, males are extremely rare. For stick insects such as the Spiny Stick Insect (*Extatosoma tiaratum*), females produce offspring of both sexes after mating but can produce females without having to mate.

Each female can produce many hundreds of eggs, usually dropping them onto the leaf litter from high in the trees and leaving them to fend for themselves. Some species deposit their eggs in the soil or attach them to tree trunks. Stick insect eggs have a hard shell that protects them during their incubation period, ranging from a couple of months to several years. The eggs of many species are camouflaged to resemble gum nuts or other plant seeds.

Left: The Spiny Stick Insect curls its abdomen over its back, mimicking the behaviour of a scorpion to deter predators.

Bottom, left: Stick insect eggs may take up to two years to hatch. They are covered in a tough shell that protects them from predators and from harsh weather conditions.

Below: Young stick insects sway when walking, giving the impression of a small twig swaying in the breeze.

Bugs
— super suckers

Hemiptera

Above: Many bugs are incredibly colourful. Jewel bugs can be found in Australian tropical rainforests.

Far right: Many shield bugs are brown or grey to blend in with tree bark. Others can be quite colourful.

Class: Insecta
Order: Hemiptera

The name "bug" is often used to cover all insects, but it is also the proper name for a particular group of insects. These insects, sometimes called "true bugs", belong to the order Hemiptera, which translates as "half-wings" and refers to the fact that a bug's wings do not usually cover its whole body. True bugs are an extremely diverse group of insects and, whether they feed on plants or animals, bugs are characterised by having piercing and sucking mouthparts.

ABOUT 100 DIFFERENT bug families are found in Australia, including cicadas, aphids, leafhoppers, assassin bugs, shield bugs, water striders and bed bugs. Families that are well adapted to living on gum trees, such as lerp insects and eurymelid bugs, are particularly common and widespread. About 98% of Australia's cicadas are found nowhere else in the world.

the FACTS!

THE GIANT Water Bug (*Lethocerus insulanus*) is the largest bug in Australia with a body length of 75 mm.

THE DOUBLE DRUMMER Cicada (*Thopha saccata*) from New South Wales and Queensland has a wingspan of 130 mm. It is not only the largest cicada in Australia, but also the loudest.

SHIELD BUGS (below) and Stink Bugs may be able to defend themselves with evil-smelling liquids that, for some species, can stain and burn human skin.

MANY BUGS have been accidentally introduced into Australia. Of the 118 known aphid species now in Australia, only eight species are definitely native.

LIKE MOSQUITOES, some bugs are known to spread disease with their piercing mouthparts. Aphids can spread diseases from one plant to another and bed bugs are known to spread diseases in humans.

A BUG FOR ALL OCCASIONS

Because they are such a diverse range of insects, bugs demonstrate many different lifestyles. Plant feeders such as aphids (left), lerp insects, scale insects and whiteflies produce honeydew as a by-product of their feeding activities. This sugary substance is collected and eaten by ants and other insects that protect their hosts against predators in return for this favour. Some ant queens even carry scale insects in their mandibles when they leave the nest to mate, to begin a new population of scale insects when they start a new nest.

Some bugs show a remarkable variety of shapes and lifestyles within a single species. Aphids, for example, may be winged or wingless and can reproduce with or without mating, depending on environmental factors. Some aphids even give birth to live young, enabling their populations to increase dramatically in a very short time.

Many bugs make a successful living in water. Giant water bugs, water boatmen, backswimmers and Water Scorpions (*Laccotrephes tristis*) have all successfully colonised freshwater streams and ponds. In particular, the water strider (*Halobates* spp.), is the only insect to have colonised the open ocean, skating across the water surface to feed on small trapped prey.

Hemiptera

THE SOUNDS OF SUMMER

The Greengrocer or Yellow Monday Cicada (*Cyclochila australasiae*) is commonly seen and heard in eastern Australia during summer. Female cicadas lay their eggs in small twigs of their host plants and the tiny nymphs drop to the ground where they feed on plant roots. The cicada nymph may live underground for seven years or more, emerging during late spring to find a mate and die after only a couple of weeks. The cast nymphal skins left by cicadas as they moult into adulthood are a common sight on fences and tree trunks. Only male cicadas sing, using special plates (tymbals) underneath the abdomen. The Bladder Cicada (*Cystosoma saundersii*) has a greatly enlarged abdomen to increase the volume of its sound.

Above, left to right: Green Leafhoppers are common on garden plants — when disturbed, they fly off almost too quickly for our eyes to follow; Certain types of whitefly nymph cover themselves with a waxy substance that may help protect them from predators; The Crusader Bug feeds on plant shoots, causing the tips to wilt — it is named after the cross on its back; Shield bugs have a solid scutellum covering their abdomens and wings and are usually patterned with bright metallic spots.

the FACTS!

SOME ASSASSIN BUGS are known to spread Chagas' disease, which caused Charles Darwin to be ill for much of his adult life. In Australia, the only assassin bug capable of doing this lives on Cape York Peninsula.

SPIT BUG NYMPHS surround themselves when feeding with a thick white frothy substance, which protects them from predators. The substance resembles human spit hanging from a branch.

CICADAS are sometimes wrongly called "locusts", which are in fact a type of grasshopper.

THE PRIMITIVE "hairy cicadas", which still exist in the cool regions of Australia, are known from fossils up to 200 million years old.

SHORE BUGS live on the edges of freshwater ponds and the seashore. One species is found on the Great Barrier Reef living on intertidal coral platforms.

GOOD BUGS & BAD BUGS

Because of their sap-sucking habits, many bugs are pests of commercial crops and garden plants. Perhaps the best known of these are the aphids, but lygaeid bugs may attack seeds and shield bugs such as the Green Vegetable Bug (*Nezara viridula*) may be serious pests of fruits. Whiteflies, mealybugs and scale insects attack a range of crops in greenhouses, but most can be controlled to some extent with their own natural predators and parasites. On the other hand, many bugs have been imported into Australia to successfully control weeds and pest insects. Perhaps some of the most beneficial bugs are scale insects that produce the dye cochineal and natural shellac, used to varnish furniture.

Above: This cicada has just emerged from its nymphal skin. Like all true bugs, its life cycle does not include a pupa.

Right: Assassin bugs come in many shapes and sizes. Unlike the majority of bugs (which are herbivorous), assassin bugs are predatory.

Grasshoppers & crickets
— Aussie jumpers

Class: Insecta
Order: Orthoptera

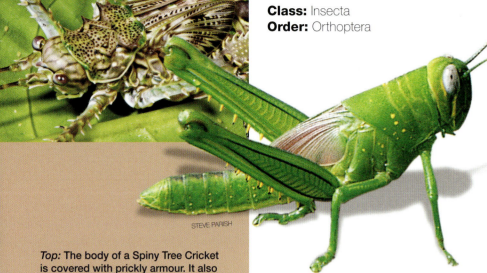

Top: The body of a Spiny Tree Cricket is covered with prickly armour. It also has powerful spiny hindlegs.

Above, right: Although adult Giant Grasshoppers are dull brown, the nymphs are bright green and also have a red and blue phase.

Grasshoppers, locusts, crickets and katydids all belong to the order Orthoptera, which is Greek for "straight wings" and refers to the shape of the forewings. As a group, these insects are known as orthopterans. Australia has a remarkable abundance of orthopterans, particularly grasshoppers, which are well adapted to its unique conditions. More than 90% of Australia's grasshoppers are found nowhere else in the world.

GRASSHOPPERS AND LOCUSTS are able to survive in unfavourable conditions and are therefore one of the most common creatures in the Australian outback. Many species can survive long dry periods in the egg stage, in which they remain dormant until years later when rain falls again. The eggs are laid in the soil and the majority of species complete their life cycle within a year. All grasshoppers feed on plants and chew leaves with their strong mandibles. They are also very active insects and most are powerful jumpers.

CRICKETS & KATYDIDS

Most crickets are plant-feeders but some are scavengers and a number of groups are predatory. The best known crickets are field crickets and mole crickets, which are often heard in suburban backyards calling in the evening. Australia's crickets are diverse, from king crickets living in rainforests to raspy crickets living in bunches of leaves tied together with silk and humpbacked crickets living in caves on the Nullarbor Plain.

Katydids are often green and tend to be perfect mimics of leaves, particularly gum leaves. They feed on leaves and flowers, but a few specialise on pollen, nectar or fruit. Katydids are excellent singers.

the FACTS!

A SINGLE SWARM of locusts may contain several billion individuals and weigh more than 70,000 tonnes.

THE NAME "LOCUST" is used for grasshoppers that spend most of their lives on their own, but which may collect into large numbers to form migratory swarms.

ORTHOPTERANS range in size from less than 5 mm to more than 100 mm. Some of the smallest and biggest grasshoppers in the world live in Australia.

THE OVIPOSITOR, used for laying eggs, is often curved like a sabre. The ovipositors of some female katydids may be twice as long as their bodies.

THE EARS of katydids and crickets are located on each foreleg, just below the knee. On many species they are small but easily visible.

A SOUND FOR ALL OCCASIONS

Orthopterans are well-known for producing sound, which may be used in defence, to establish territory, to gather other orthopterans into swarms or to attract a mate. Depending on the species, they pick up these sounds either with eardrums on the legs or thorax, or through special hairs on different parts of the body.

Above: The populations of wingless grasshoppers can boom when conditions are favourable — and they may become pests.

Other insects
— the less-known groups

SILVERFISH — SCALY INSECTS

Silverfish (order Thysanura) are one of the most primitive insect groups. All members of the group are wingless and are covered with silvery scales from which they derive their name. Silverfish live over most of Australia in a wide range of habitats; they feed mostly on plants and rotting organic matter. A few species live in ant or termite nests.

EARWIGS — EARLY WINGS

Earwigs (order Dermaptera) have a pair of pincers (cerci) at the end of the abdomen. These may be used for defence or to hold food. They have two pairs of wings — short, toughened forewings and larger, transparent hindwings. The hindwings are used in flight and are ear-shaped, giving them their original name of "ear-wing". Earwigs generally live under bark or stones and feed on organic matter such as dead leaves.

STONEFLIES — FLYING LIKE A STONE

Stoneflies (order Plecoptera) are similar to mayflies but have long bodies and wings that are folded flat against the body when at rest. The adults are generally found near water and feed on rotting wood and algae. The nymphs spend their entire development under water.

Above, top to bottom: The introduced silverfish is common in most homes in Australia — it doesn't survive well in areas away from humans; Female earwigs generally protect their eggs until they hatch; they defend themselves and their eggs with their long pincers (cerci); Adult stoneflies are not commonly seen, rarely moving far from waterways.

COCKROACHES — UNLOVED BUT IMPORTANT

Cockroaches (order Blattodea, right) come in many sizes but all have their heads covered by part of the thorax. Most are wingless, or only the males are winged and some species are blind. They live mainly under bark or logs, feeding on rotting wood or other organic matter. The diet of almost all species is unknown. A few species are introduced to Australia, but there are more than 400 native species that are very important components of natural ecosystems.

MAYFLIES — ONE-DAY WONDERS

Mayflies (order Ephemeroptera, left) are found around water. The nymphs live under water feeding on aquatic vplants. They have large branching gills on the abdomen and may moult 20 times or more before reaching adulthood. Adult mayflies are short-lived and do not feed. They collect in large swarms around fresh water to mate in mid-flight, then females leave to lay eggs into the water. The nymphs may take anywhere from a few months to a few years to mature.

the FACTS!

MANY FISH and freshwater invertebrate species feed on young stoneflies. Consequently, female stoneflies lay vast numbers of eggs, more than 1000 at a time.

ADULT MAYFLIES have a pair of claspers (gonostyles) located at the end of the abdomen. These are used to hold onto their partner during mating.

A FAST COCKROACH can run at about 40 body-lengths per second. Humans can run at about four body-lengths per second.

Other orders

Above: Like some other types of insects, webspinners produce silk. However, these insects produce it from the tips of their forelegs.

Right: All scorpionflies can be predatory. The way that this one carries its caterpillar prey is characteristic.

Bottom: Caddisflies are generally dull-coloured insects that are similar to moths. They are rarely noticed.

SCORPIONFLIES — NOT SCORPIONS, NOT FLIES

Scorpionflies (order Mecoptera) look similar to true flies but possess two pairs of wings instead of one. The adults are sometimes predatory, particularly males, but mostly feed on nectar, pollen and fruit. Eggs are laid in the soil. Larvae are either aquatic or live in mud, so scorpionflies are generally restricted to cooler moist parts of coastal Australia.

the FACTS!

THE WEB-SPINNING ORGANS on the forelegs of webspinners may contain up to 200 silk glands. These insects are able to spin silk as soon as they hatch from the egg.

THE WORLD'S ONLY marine caddisfly (*Philanisus plebeius*), lives in rock pools in New Zealand and southern Australia.

SCORPIONFLIES are named for the characteristic way some males fly — with the abdomen curled up like a scorpion. They also may have a pair of tail claws that resemble a scorpion's tail.

THE RARE ANTLION LACEWING (*Heoclisis fulva*) from northern and central Australia has a wingspan of 150 mm and is the country's largest.

WEBSPINNERS — SELDOM SEEN SPINNERS

Webspinners (order Embioptera) are a small group of insects that are rarely seen. They spin silken galleries under bark or in soil or leaf litter, feeding on plant material within the gallery. Eggs are laid in the galleries and protected by the female. Only the males are winged and they are short-lived, dying soon after mating.

CADDISFLIES — INSect FISHING NETS

Caddisflies (order Trichoptera) are small, moth-like insects whose wings are covered with hair rather than scales. The larvae are aquatic and construct small cases from fragments of plants or sand. Some species are predatory and build small silken nets to trap prey moving downstream; other species feed on plants. The mouthparts of the adults are modified to feed only on liquids such as water.

LACEWINGS — INSECT IMPALERS

Both adult and larval lacewings (order Neuroptera) are predatory, feeding mostly on soft-bodied insects such as aphids. The larvae possess a large pair of hollow, pincer-like jaws at the front of the head, with which they impale their prey and suck out the juices. Antlions are a group of lacewings whose larvae dig cone-shaped pits in loose sand to trap passing ants, impaling them as they tumble down the side of the pit.

Right, top to bottom: The antlion larva bears a large pair of hollow jaws to impale any insect that falls into its pit; Mantispid lacewings look similar to praying mantids. They have a similar way of life, although the lacewing larvae are parasitic.

Inheritors of the Earth
— why so many insects?

Of all the animals that have ever existed on Earth, insects are by far the most successful; they were present 200 million years before the dinosaurs appeared and will probably survive well after humans have gone. Insects have successfully dominated every freshwater and terrestrial environment on Earth and their success and abundance is due to a number of factors.

Above: Under ideal conditions, caterpillars can build up large populations that can devastate young trees; however, their populations are mostly well controlled.

Above: Ants have an efficient and functional social system that enables them to grow enormous nests when enough food is available.

FIVE KEY REASONS

FIRSTLY, their small size enables them to exploit many different resources. Each gum tree, for example, can house and feed thousands of individual insects. Their life cycle also enables them to divide up food within a single lifetime, so that, for example, caterpillars live on plants and feed on leaves, whereas butterflies fly through the air and feed on flowers.

SECONDLY, their ability to reproduce is phenomenal. Whereas most animals require months or at least weeks to reproduce, some insects can reproduce within hours of being born and each female can produce thousands of offspring.

THIRDLY, in comparison to other invertebrates, insects have a well-developed, highly-organised nervous system, enabling them to respond to subtle daily changes in the environment. Some are also able to organise into massive colonies with advanced social structures and communication systems.

FOURTHLY, insects are the only invertebrates with wings. These enable them to avoid non-flying predators, reach food sources high up in the trees and disperse long distances, including across oceans.

FINALLY, the lives of many insects are intimately linked to the lives of other plants and animals and continue that way through the process of co-evolution. This process has resulted in the production of thousands of diverse insect species, linked to the plants and animals on which they depend.

the FACTS!

INSECTS CAN COLONISE new habitats very quickly. Studies showed that, after a volcano erupted on the island of Montserrat, up to 30 kg of insects arrived on the fresh landscape every day.

LADYBIRDS (*Hippodamia convergens*) congregate in caves to "overwinter" each year. These congregations may contain up to 42 million individuals.

THE DENSITY OF WEEVILS (*Sitona discoideus*) in the soil of improved pasture may be 200 larvae in each double handful of soil.

ONE HECTARE of improved pasture, which is not a particularly diverse habitat, may contain nearly eighteen million individual beetles.

IT HAS BEEN ESTIMATED that there are more than 200 million individual insects for each human on Earth. This adds up to about one quintillion insects (ten with eighteen noughts following).

THE WORLD'S INSECTS weigh about 27.5 billion tonnes, approximately six times the weight of the world's human population.

Below: Some colonies of termites may contain more than one million workers.

HOW MANY ARE THERE?

Scientists do not know how many insect species there are in the world because most of them have not yet been described; however, they do know that about 90% of all living animal species are insects. Vertebrates, including all mammals, birds, reptiles, frogs and fishes, make up only 2% of the Earth's total animal species.

Getting through life
— insect life cycles

Above: A fully fed Orchard Butterfly caterpillar, preparing to pupate.

The insect empire is divided into the wingless insects (silverfish and bristletails) and the winged insects (all others). The winged insects are further divided into two groups based on their life cycles.

THE MORE PRIMITIVE group (the hemimetabola) has a life cycle that proceeds directly from egg to adult, without a metamorphosis. The young insects are all small, wingless versions of the adults. This group includes, among others, dragonflies, stick insects, cockroaches, mantids, grasshoppers and bugs.

Left, clockwise from top left: Beekiller Assassin Bug nymphs hatching from a mass of eggs; A nymph that has moulted twice since hatching; A nymph in the act of moulting; An adult, fully winged assassin bug.

the FACTS!

THE BREATHING SYSTEM of an insect (trachea) is actually part of the exoskeleton. So when insects moult, they must withdraw these tubes from throughout the body and replace them with new ones.

DURING MOULTING, insects suck in air or water to make their bodies as large as possible while the new skin hardens. Afterwards, the air or water is released to make room for the insect to grow.

BOTH BUTTERFLIES and moths form a pupa (or chrysalis) as the third stage of the life cycle. Many moths protect themselves by spinning a cocoon in which to pupate. Butterflies, however, never form cocoons.

MANY INSECTS consume all the food they need as a larva and do not need to feed as adults. Others, such as butterflies, require only sugar for energy to fly.

Below: Eggs and nymphs of the Bronze Orange Bug. Note that both older and younger nymphs are still clustering around eggs.

THE YOUNG INSECTS of the second group (the holometabola) are completely different from the adults and are transformed from larva to adult by metamorphosis as a pupa, often inside a cocoon. For example, caterpillars transform into butterflies, maggots become flies, beetle grubs become adult beetles. This second group is far larger than the first group and also includes fleas, lacewings, moths, ants, bees and wasps. It includes almost 90% of insect species.

Above, clockwise from top left: Orchard Butterfly eggs laid on the leaf of a lemon tree; A young caterpillar (mimicking a bird dropping); The Orchard Butterfly pupa mimics the colour of its surroundings; A newly emerged male Orchard Butterfly expanding its wings.

HERE FOR A SHORT TIME

The length of an insect's life cycle varies between species and groups, but most species in cooler areas cannot survive winter, and die within twelve to eighteen months of birth. Activity is generally greatest during spring and summer. The harsher winter period, particularly in southern Australia, is spent inactively, usually in the egg stage. The larval stage usually comprises the longest part of the insect's life cycle.

Above, left to right: Insects such as crickets moult at night to hide from predators because they are at their most vulnerable during this stage; Adult Orchard Butterflies mating; Assassin bugs mating.

Left: An adult Greengrocer Cicada emerging from its nymphal skin. The entire process may take two hours or more.

ENDURING NYMPHS

The Greengrocer Cicada (*Cyclochila australasiae*) spends seven years underground as a nymph but dies after only a few weeks as an adult. Mayfly adults may live less than a day, after spending a year or more as a nymph in fast-flowing streams. The entire life cycle of other insects spans only a few days or weeks, but queen termites may live for many years.

THE SMALL STAY SMALL

Because adult insects no longer moult, they remain the same size. The size of the adult Bush Fly (*Musca vetustissima*) is determined by the amount and quality of food eaten as a maggot. There are not different types of Bush Flies, just different sizes. Very small ones appear when too many maggots feed together on a single food source, such as a cow pat.

INSECT MOULTING

Because the skeleton of an insect is on the outside of the body instead of the inside (like ours), a young insect must shed its hard protective covering, called an exoskeleton, in order to grow. This is done by moulting. Moulting usually takes place at night or in a protected space because the insect is very soft and sluggish immediately afterwards and vulnerable to predators. The insect first takes air into its body to increase its size as much as possible, then the old skin splits down the back and the insect extracts itself. The new skin usually requires several hours to dry before the insect is free to move off.

Most insects moult three to seven times, but some species undergo as many as 40 moults. All insects must moult as nymphs or larvae, but moulting ceases upon reaching adulthood. The exceptions are mayflies, which moult once more immediately after becoming adults, while springtails and bristletails keep moulting throughout adult life.

In the second group of insects, the holometabola, individuals undergo a special type of moult, called metamorphosis, before becoming adult. Metamorphosis is a form of moulting where, instead of a simple increase in size, the larva undergoes a complete transformation into adulthood. The larval body, including the internal tissues, is completely destroyed and the adult body is built in its place.

Left: Newly hatched shield bugs still clustering in a group around their empty eggs.

the FACTS!

MOULTING BEGINS when an insect produces "moulting fluid" under the old exoskeleton. This breaks down the inner layers and makes the outer layers easier to shed. The moulting fluid and the inner layers of the old exoskeleton are re-absorbed.

MOULTING may be triggered by an insect's size, age, hormones or environment. Most commonly it is a combination of all these factors.

INSECTS GENERALLY REQUIRE high humidity in which to moult properly. If the air is too dry, the insect may get stuck in its old skin.

THE INCREASE IN SIZE from egg to adult varies between insect species. Some aphids increase their weight by only sixteen times, whereas slow-growing caterpillars may increase by an amazing 72,000 times.

JUVENILE INSECTS with an incomplete metamorphosis are generally called nymphs. Those with a complete metamorphosis are called larvae.

PAEDOGENESIS is an unusual adaptation whereby juvenile insects are able to reproduce without needing to mature into adulthood. Some gall midges, beetles and a few other insects demonstrate this.

Insects that disappear
— camouflage

Above: Many types of grasshopper are patterned to blend in with leaf litter on the forest floor.

Centre: Looper Moths sit with their wings flat against tree bark and are true masters of disguise.

Many insects hide or flee to avoid being eaten by predators, but those that stay out in the open need to use other methods to avoid detection. Consequently, insects may use camouflage to make themselves apparently disappear altogether. Camouflage involves the use of colour, body shape and behaviour to resemble leaves, flowers, bark, stones and even bird droppings.

NOW YOU SEE ME, NOW YOU DON'T

Camouflaged insects are often two-toned; a dark colour on top conceals them against the ground when seen from above and a paler one underneath camouflages them against the sky when seen from below. Many butterflies can choose whether or not to be camouflaged. With their wings open, bright colours are used to attract the opposite sex; with their wings closed, only the dull brown underside can be seen and the butterfly disappears into the background.

ECO ILLUSIONISTS

Many types of moth, particularly geometrid or looper moths (left), have intricately patterned wings that are held flat when resting on trees to blend perfectly with the pattern of the bark. Other moths are the exact shape, colour and pattern of dead leaves, with lines resembling leaf veins that make them invisible when resting among leaf litter. Insects such as caterpillars, which imitate bark or twigs, often have flanges or hair on the sides of the body to eliminate shadows that could give them away to predators.

UNDERCOVER ATTACK

Not all camouflage is used to hide from predators. Mantids, for example, use camouflage to ambush insects that feed on flowers and leaves. Their green (or sometimes brown) bodies and gentle swaying movements disguise their approach from unwary prey. Assassin bugs, which impale their prey on the end of a long proboscis (rostrum), may also be superbly camouflaged.

Many insects camouflage themselves so ingeniously that they are invisible to an observer only centimetres away. It is a very successful strategy and so is used by a great range of insects. Moth and butterfly caterpillars, bugs such as leafhoppers, beetles such as weevils, grasshoppers, crickets and katydids all excel at disappearing.

Above, right: This black leafhopper bug has the perfect camouflage on a burnt log.

Left: Green Mantid.

the FACTS!

SOME INSECTS are actually able to change their colour to suit their background. This is a complicated process and can take several minutes to several hours.

A SINGLE INSECT may utilise different types of camouflage at different ages. A young caterpillar may be green to resemble leaves; the older caterpillar may be long and brown to resemble twigs. The pupa may look like a dried leaf and the adult moth may be mottled to resemble bark.

SOME CATERPILLARS suddenly produce a fleshy red organ from the back of the head to frighten predators when their camouflage is no longer effective. This organ is called an "osmeterium".

THE STICK-SHAPED body, brown colour and gentle swaying movements of stick insects blend them perfectly with their surroundings and help them avoid detection by predators.

SOME GREEN KATYDID species that feed on gum trees also have a reddish tinge to their legs, similar to the reddish tinge on the stems of gum leaves.

The great pretenders
— mimicry

Mimicry is similar to camouflage except the insects resemble a particular object rather than disappearing into the general background. Harmless insects often mimic poisonous or more aggressive ones, but they will also mimic a range of living animals and objects.

MORE THAN SKIN DEEP

Mimicry is most commonly recognised by the physical resemblance to another insect or object, but it can also involve copying behaviour, chemicals or sounds. Some beetles such as checkered beetles (below) will mimic the behaviour of wasps, which may include walking rapidly, stopping frequently and waving of the antennae to try to convince predators to leave them alone. Intruders into ant nests may use their front legs to mimic the way ants tap each other's antennae in order to recognise nest mates and thus pass through unharmed.

Other insects, particularly bugs, may produce the same type of chemicals used by ants and so smell like an ant, even if they don't particularly look like one. Some beetles produce a loud buzzing sound as they fly, similar to a large wasp, so birds will think twice before attacking.

The heads of some caterpillars may be designed to look like a creature that would attack potential predators. Hawk moth caterpillars sometimes have an enlarged area behind the head with eye-like patterns that would make a bird think it was face to face with another predator.

Above: Tiger moths are a group of moths that all display warning colours. They are all thought to be poisonous.

Above: The rear end of a Hercules Moth caterpillar bears an uncanny resemblance to the face of a frog.

Bottom, right: Newly hatched Spiny Stick Insect nymphs mimic a local ant that most predators avoid.

the FACTS!

ANTS MAY MIMIC the behaviour or smell of termites to get inside a termite colony and eat the workers.

SOME CATERPILLARS are big enough to mimic small snakes. The caterpillar has a pair of eye-shaped spots on the back of its head that it flashes when disturbed. These eye spots have slit pupils, like a snake's.

INSECTS MAY NOT NEED to be accurate mimics. Sometimes they only need to mimic a particular aspect of another animal in order to deter predators.

MIMICRY is not only used to avoid being eaten. Some predatory insects mimic others to attract prey, luring male insects to their deaths by imitating the smells emitted by females of that species.

THE WANDERER BUTTERFLY is poisonous and is mimicked by many other butterfly species, including Lesser Wanderers, Danaid Eggflies and Viceroy Butterflies.

A SUCCESSFUL COMBINATION

Some insects use both camouflage and mimicry in combination. A number of predatory insects will camouflage themselves to avoid predators, but use mimicry to catch their prey. Others change from camouflage to mimicry (or vice versa) as they grow. The nymph of the Spiny Stick Insect mimics a local species of red-headed ant when very young, going as far as curling its abdomen over to look more like an ant's abdomen. As it grows too big to be an ant, the nymph turns green-brown and relies on its camouflage to survive.

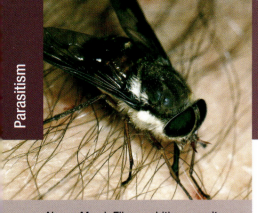

Above: March Flies are biting parasites that are well known to people who live near the coast.

Centre: An aphid wasp moves among its prey. During its life it will lay eggs in a large number of aphids.

Living inside others
— parasitism

Although the majority of insects feed on plants, almost one in every ten insect species leads a parasitic way of life. Some, such as fleas and lice, are parasitic on humans and other vertebrates, but the majority of insect parasites live out their lives inside the bodies of other insects. These parasites only use one host and eventually kill that host. They are known as parasitoids.

MOST INSECT PARASITOIDS are either flies or wasps. Their major hosts are beetles, moths and butterflies, but they will also attack other insect groups, as well as worms, snails and spiders.

The parasitoid's eggs are usually laid on or into the body of the host, or may be laid on leaves that are later eaten by the host. The parasitoid larvae hatch and burrow through the body of the host, selectively feeding on its internal organs so it stays alive as long as possible. The host continues feeding and developing, initially showing no outward sign of the infesting parasitoid, but eventually dies once the parasitoid is fully fed. Then the parasitoid pupates and emerges as an adult.

the FACTS!

ALMOST EVERY INSECT species is attacked by parasitoids. While some insects have no known parasitoids, others support more than 50 species.

TREE-DWELLING insects support the largest numbers of parasitoids, and the majority of parasitoid–host interactions exist between parasitic wasps and caterpillars.

PARASITES MAY BE SEEN in your own garden. Aphids are commonly parasitised by tiny wasps that make the aphids die and turn brown. These aphid "mummies" remain fixed among groups of live aphids.

PLANTS UNDER ATTACK from caterpillars may produce chemicals that attract parasitic wasps. The wasps in turn attack the caterpillars, helping the plants survive.

VERY SMALL WASPS parasitise the eggs of other insects. Forty or more wasp larvae may develop inside a single butterfly egg.

ADULT PARASITIC WASPS and flies do not themselves generally feed on other insects. Instead they usually drink nectar from flowers.

Right: This caterpillar is an empty shell. It has been eaten out by wasp larvae that have formed white cocoons outside the caterpillar's body.

FINDING A VICTIM

Many parasitoid species are very specific and will attack only hosts of a particular species or group of species. They generally employ very sophisticated methods to locate hosts, such as using the smell produced by a plant when its leaves are being eaten by caterpillars, or following the mating pheromones produced by female insects to attract males.

Other parasitoids are attracted to the host's dung or even its body heat. Some wasps can locate beetle grubs that burrow in wood because the temperature of the bark close to the grub is one degree higher than the surrounding bark. The wasp will then drill its ovipositor through the wood and lay an egg on the hapless grub. Because parasitoids often find hosts by initially locating a habitat (such as tree trunks, flowers or roots), the number of parasitoid species that attack any particular host largely depends on where that host lives.

Above, left to right: Wallaby Flies, as their name suggests, live in the fur of wallabies, sucking their blood; The whitish grub on the right is a fly larva that has been feeding on the sawfly larva on the left. When fully fed, the fly larva will pupate into an adult; Parasitic wasps may be so small that they grow up feeding inside a single praying mantid egg — this one has just emerged from the mantid egg sac.

FIGHTING BACK

Because the great majority of insects that attack others are parasitoids rather than predators, insect defences are more geared towards avoiding parasitoids than predators. For many species, the major cause of death in any population is attack by parasitoids. Parasitoid eggs are laid on host insects at all stages in the life cycle, but hosts use an array of defences to try to prevent infection or to kill the parasitoid once infection has occurred. For example, when a wasp or fly lands on a caterpillar's back, the caterpillar swings its head wildly to knock the parasitoid away. If an egg is laid on a caterpillar's body, it can often twist around and use its mouthparts to remove the egg once the parasitoid has gone. Consequently, parasitoids tend to lay their eggs just behind the caterpillar's head, out of reach of its mouthparts. Some caterpillars destroy wasp parasitoids by surrounding them with tissue and starving them of oxygen.

Left: These leaf beetle larvae have had white eggs attached to them by a parasitic fly.

the FACTS!

POLYEMBRYONY occurs when a parasitic wasp's egg starts to divide after it is laid into a host. This may produce more than 400 eggs that hatch into wasp larvae which then devour their host.

A NUMBER of different types of parasites attack aphids. However, the aphids receive protection from ants that drive the parasites away. In return, the aphids provide sweet honeydew for the ants.

"HYPERPARASITES" are parasitic wasps or flies that parasitise other species of parasitic wasps or flies. This usually involves very small parasitic wasps attacking larger wasps and flies.

INSECTS SUCH AS LICE that parasitise mammals and birds are parasitic throughout their lives. Insects that parasitise other insects are only parasitic in the larval stages of their life cycle.

OF THE 120,000 or so known species of parasitic insects in the world, almost 90% are wasps. The rest are flies, beetles, moths and a small group called strepsipterans.

THE PARASITE ARMS RACE

Wasps in particular have developed weapons to overcome the defences of their hosts. Some caterpillars live underground and are parasitised by stout wasps with strong digging legs. Other caterpillars hide during the day and feed at night but are attacked by nocturnal parasitic wasps. Caterpillars that feed on leaves drop from the plant on a silken thread when a wasp is nearby, but the wasp climbs down the thread after them.

Grubs that feed in wood are attacked by wasps with small flattened bodies and short legs that follow the grubs through tunnels in the wood. Many caterpillars have stinging hairs or spines for defence, but very small species of wasps can move among the stinging hairs of the hosts to lay their eggs unharmed. Some caterpillars spin very tough cocoons that are parasitised by determined wasps with corkscrew-like ovipositors.

Right: The Blue Ant is actually a wingless wasp that lays its eggs on mole crickets.

Insects helping us
— beneficial insects

Above: Ladybird larvae can be very effective in controlling aphids and other pests in gardens.

Right: There are hundreds of different species of Australian native wasp that are important plant pollinators.

The great majority of insects do not cause humans any harm and may be directly or indirectly beneficial to us.

WITHOUT INSECTS, humans would probably become extinct on Earth within six months. Insects pollinate a great proportion of our food, they keep nutrients cycling and prevent the Earth being piled many metres high in rotting plant and animal material. Insects provide us with food, wax, silk, dyes and many pharmaceuticals. They give us models to solve problems of engineering and aerodynamics and can answer complex questions of genetics, evolution, social behaviour and organisation.

THE HIDDEN MAJORITY

When it comes to insects, most people are aware only of the few pest species that enter our homes or damage our food crops. The majority of these are introduced insects and cause problems because they are not living where they naturally belong. Alongside these are tens of thousands of native Australian insects, most of which live their lives secretively in the bush and are rarely seen. Cockroaches, for example, are best known for the two or three introduced species that infest our houses, but more than 400 native species live in bushland throughout Australia, each an important part of the natural ecosystem.

INSECTS CONTROLLING INSECTS (& PLANTS)

A natural enemy of a pest insect or weed may be imported as a helpful "biological control" — but only after years of testing to ensure it won't become a pest too. The natural enemy, or a suite of them, should bring pest numbers below the level where they cause harm to the environment.

BETTER OFF WITH THEM

Insects are not only directly beneficial to humans, but to the Earth as a whole (and therefore indirectly beneficial to us). They keep the plants of the world growing by pollinating flowers and dispersing seeds. Most vertebrates rely on insects for some part of their diet and in many parts of the world humans still cook and eat a range of insects. Everyone in Australia also consumes insects, but we tend to ingest small fragments of beetles and caterpillars in our fruits and vegetables, rather than actively seeking them as a food source like people in other countries.

Above: These leaf beetles have been introduced to Australia to control Boneseed, a serious environmental weed in many coastal areas.

the FACTS!

THE AUSTRALIAN ABORIGINES included at least nineteen different species of insect in their diet. These insects provided essential nutrients such as vitamin C. Scurvy outbreaks occurred when certain insects became scarce.

INSECTS CAN BE NUTRITIOUS. 100 g of beetles produces more than 2000 kJ of energy, whereas 100 g of beef produces only 530 kJ. Witchetty Grubs contain almost 50% protein but are also 50% fat.

INSECTS HAVE BEEN USED for many years as medicines. A variety of pulverised insects have been used to cure toothaches and the heads of ants or beetles have been used to close wounds. South American Indians used the jaws of beetles to hold the two edges of a wound together, afterwards pulling the head off so it remained in place until the wound healed.

MOST AUSTRALIANS are aware of the introduced European Wasp, but are unaware of the 10,000 native Australian wasp species that control insect pests and pollinate both native plants and agricultural crops.

Them versus us
— insects & humans

It has been estimated that only 0.15% of insect species are harmful in any way to humans, whereas humans are harmful to almost all insect species. However, those insects that are harmful can sometimes take a heavy toll on us and our food supplies.

Left: Blowfly maggots massing in composting kitchen waste. Blowflies are able to produce enormous populations in a very short time.

Above: Christmas beetles are one of the few insects that have apparently increased in number due to Europeans changing the landscape.

THE BATTLE FOR FOOD

The battle between insects and humans stretches back thousands of years to when humans first altered the landscape enough to allow plagues of insects to occur. Selective breeding of crops over thousands of years has bred out most of the plants' natural defences. These defences included toxic chemicals and tough leaves that made them less palatable to humans as well as insects.

Also, plants such as wild wheat have a natural tendency to grow over wide areas mixed in with other vegetation for a short period of time, making it difficult for plant-eating insects to track them down. Humans now plant fields of defenceless crops year after year over hundreds of square kilometres. These fields promote insect populations by providing them with an unlimited food source. A similar problem applies to cattle, sheep and other stock that are attacked by insect pests.

Above: A number of different types of caterpillars feed on cabbages. Their feeding can do severe damage.

KEEPING THEM UNDER CONTROL

Native insects can become pests if humans alter the landscape; or insects from overseas become pests when they are introduced accidentally or on purpose — without their natural enemies. Preventing unwanted introductions is the work of the national quarantine services. For insect problems that already exist though, humans have developed hundreds of different types of chemical insecticides. But insects rapidly evolve resistance to insecticides (making the chemicals ineffective), and the insecticides cause ongoing problems to the environment and to humans. One long-term answer may be "biological control": the use of the insects' natural predators, parasites and diseases.

Biological control, when successful, eliminates the need for excessive use of chemicals and should keep the pest under control forever, especially when used as one of several control methods. The challenge for science lies in ensuring that the newly imported insects do their job well — and without any negative consequences for native ecosystems.

Right: Of the more than 150 species of aphids in Australia, only a small proportion are thought to be native. Most species are considered pests.

the FACTS!

INTRODUCED PESTS may spread at different rates. The weevil (*Sitona discoideus*) has spread through southern Australia at about 150 km per year, probably under its own power, whereas the Egyptian Beetle (*Blaps polychresta*) has spread only 2 km per year, and that is probably with the help of humans.

ALL CROP PLANTS are attacked by insects and in the worst cases they may consume up to 60% of the harvest — leaving only 40% for human consumption.

SUGAR CANE alone is attacked by 1350 different insect pest species around the world.

INTRODUCED INSECTS are well suited to living with us and our food sources and make up about half of all insect species living in suburban areas and on farmland.

WHEN EUROPEANS first arrived in Australia, they accidentally brought a variety of insect pests with them and, despite strict quarantine rules, many more continue to arrive today.

Making more insects
— reproduction

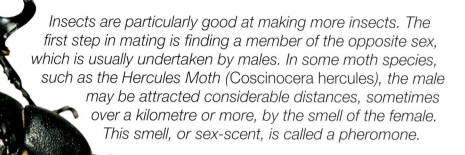

Insects are particularly good at making more insects. The first step in mating is finding a member of the opposite sex, which is usually undertaken by males. In some moth species, such as the Hercules Moth (*Coscinocera hercules*), the male may be attracted considerable distances, sometimes over a kilometre or more, by the smell of the female. This smell, or sex-scent, is called a pheromone.

the FACTS!

THE INSECT that produces the fewest eggs over its lifetime is probably the Louse Fly (*Hippobosca variegata*), with an average of fewer than five.

THE AUSTRALIAN Ghost Moth (*Trictena atripalpis*) is capable of producing more than 44,000 eggs during its short life. The world record holder, however, is probably the African Driver Ant (*Dorylus wilverthi*) queen: she can lay more than 100 million eggs during her lifetime.

WHETHER AN EGG HATCHES into a male or female may depend on temperature. In some mosquito species, the eggs hatch into females if the water temperature is a constant 28°C. Males are produced at lower temperatures.

IN SOCIAL INSECTS, females are produced from unfertilised eggs and males from fertilised ones.

GETTING TO KNOW EACH OTHER

In many insect species, mating begins with courtship. Courtship may involve a single male performing a dance or other feat to impress a female, or it may involve fights between males for the right to mate with a female. Males of species such as the Rhinoceros Beetle (*Xylotrupes gideon*) or Rainbow Stag Beetle (*Phalacrognathus muelleri*) may fight using horns, jaws or brute strength.

Courtship ranges from simple stroking of females by males, to the complex flying dances of butterflies. Robber flies and scorpionflies bring their female partners a gift of small insect prey. Once the female is agreeable, further complex dances may be performed by both partners before mating begins.

Above: The shiny red penis (adaegus) of a male rhinoceros beetle can be seen during mating.

Left: Grasshoppers characteristically mate with the male sitting on the back of the female.

Right: Cairns Birdwing Butterflies may continue to mate for a full day — the smaller male is carried in flight by the female.

THE ART OF MATING

Most insects mate end-to-end, facing opposite directions (below). The larger mate, usually the female, may continue to move forward and feed normally, forcing the male to run or fly backwards. Female butterflies, such as the Orchard Butterfly (*Papilio aegeus*) will continue to fly around with the male hanging limply below, attached only by the tip of the abdomen. Beetles usually mate with the male on top and both sexes facing the same direction.

Mating may take anywhere from five seconds to eleven days, depending on the species of insect and the circumstances. In a number of species, the male will guard the female from other males after mating. Some male insects will simply stay with her for up to several weeks until she lays eggs.

Above: Some cockroaches carry their egg sac, or ootheca, at the back of their abdomen until the eggs hatch.

PARENTS WITHOUT PARTNERS

In some insect groups, including stick insects, males are not necessary for reproduction and females are able to produce viable offspring on their own. This is known as parthenogenesis. Female Pear and Cherry Slugs (*Caliroa cerasi*) were accidentally introduced into Australia many years ago, but no males have yet been recorded here. Some insects have both male and female reproductive organs, giving them the opportunity to mate with themselves if members of the opposite sex are unavailable. This is the case for some populations of the Cottony Cushion Scale (*Icerya purchasi*) — an Australian bug that has become a pest overseas.

LOOKING AFTER BABY

Although most insects abandon their eggs, the females of some sawflies, shield bugs and others stand guard over an egg batch and remain there until the eggs have hatched and the nymphs moulted at least once. When the eggs are threatened, the female moves her body between the eggs and the direction of the threat and will keep shifting her position as the angle of the threat changes (right).

THE NEXT GENERATION

Although most insects lay eggs that hatch after a certain incubation period or survive for many months if not years, many insects can lay eggs that hatch as they are being laid or can even give birth to live young. The female Tsetse Fly in Africa keeps the egg inside her body until the larva hatches, then feeds it a highly nutritious milky substance prior to the actual birth. Eggs are often eaten or parasitised by other insects, so many species such as stick insects produce eggs that look like plant seeds and drop them into leaf litter where they are very difficult to see. Green Lacewings produce eggs at the tops of long stalks, which discourages cannibalism by the hatchlings. Female Mottled Cup Moths (*Doratifera vulnerans*) cover their eggs with their body scales to disguise them.

Above: A female Cruiser Butterfly laying eggs. She tests the plant with the tip of her abdomen before laying each egg.

the FACTS!

SHIELD BUGS mate end-to-end (below) and the larger female often drags the male around backwards. This is commonly seen with the Harlequin Bug.

THE MALE Wanderer Butterfly (*Danaus plexippus*) produces a pheromone that affects the operation of the female's wing muscles, making her land on a nearby branch for mating.

IN SPECIES that only mate once, the female will switch off all pheromones once she has mated.

FEMALES of the Whitefringed Weevil (*Graphognathus leucoloma*), a pest introduced into Australia from overseas, can lay more than 3000 eggs without mating.

MALE TWO-SPOTTED Flower Beetles (*Malachius bipustulatus*) have yellowish outgrowths called "excitators" on their antennae; the females feed on these growths during courtship.

Sensing their world
— insect senses

Above: The antennae of this male rhipicerid beetle are used to pick up tiny scent particles in the air.

Most insects have poor eyesight and can see only a few millimetres in any direction. Their compound eyes on each side of the head are made up of hundreds of simple eye facets that are not able to focus and can only form a simple image.

PREDATORY INSECTS such as dragonflies (below) have excellent vision with thousands of facets in eyes that comprise most of the insect's head. In many species of fly, the eyes of the males are better than those of the females to enable them to recognise and pursue females for mating.

HEARING YOUR WAY AROUND

Many insects may have poor hearing but are also able to pick up sound vibrations through hairs on the body or through the body wall. Insects such as crickets and moths also have specialised "ear drums" on their legs and abdomens.

Moths can hear the high-pitched clicks produced by insect-eating bats for echolocation. Bats use these clicks (ultrasound) to detect flying insects in the dark. Some moths fold up their wings mid-flight and drop to the ground when they hear a bat nearby. Nocturnal cockroaches, crickets, lacewings and beetles can also detect ultrasound.

THREE ORANGE ocelli can be clearly seen between the compound eyes of the Greengrocer Cicada (left). Their exact function is still unclear.

WHAT'S THAT SMELL?

Smell and taste are closely related and insects have a great range of sense organs that can do one or both. Much of their sense of smell is concentrated in the antennae, which are lined with hundreds of tiny pits for detecting particles in the air. The American Cockroach (*Periplaneta americana*) has about 100,000 of these pits on each antenna, enabling them to detect minute amounts of any odour.

Above, left: The eyes of Baron Dragonflies comprise most of the head. *Above:* Male Hercules Moth (*Coscinocera hercules*).

MORE AWARE THAN US

Compared to insects, humans have a somewhat limited sensory repertoire. Insects can sense their world in many ways, using sense organs located all over their bodies, probably in ways we are yet to imagine. Some female jewel beetles, for example, have heat-sensitive organs on their heads that lead them to small bushfires. The beetle then lays her eggs on the smouldering wood and the grubs feed on the weakened trees.

Below: White-kneed Crickets have long "palps" around their mouthparts; these are probably used as sense organs in the dark.

---

the FACTS!

THE WHIRLIGIG BEETLE (*Dineutes politus*) lives in freshwater and has two pairs of eyes — one pair that sits above the water and one pair below.

TUMBLING FLOWER beetles (*Mordella* spp.) may have 25,000 simple eyes in each of their compound eyes.

A GROUP OF SCARAB BEETLES called cockchafers use the sun as a compass. By using polarised light they can tell, even on cloudy days, where they are by the angle of the sun.

EACH ANTENNA of the male Radar Beetle (*Rhipicera* sp.) is about as wide as the beetle's body. The fan-like antennae are similar to satellite dishes and are used to detect the presence of females from long distances.

A JEWEL BEETLE (*Melanophila acuminata*) has a sensory organ that can detect the wavelengths of heat radiation from forest fires. These wavelengths are invisible to humans but can be detected by beetles up to 5 km from the fire.

Living colours
— insect colours

Above: Many wasps are brightly coloured yellow and black — the most common type of warning colours.

Below: Many grasshopper species are a dull brown or grey as adults, but are brightly coloured when young.

The natural colour of the insect exoskeleton is a dull brown, produced by the compounds that strengthen it. These compounds are absent in newly moulted insects, giving them a pale appearance that darkens as the exoskeleton hardens.

MOST INSECTS have added colour to the exoskeleton in one of two ways. The first is with microscopic structures in the outer layer, called the cuticle, which reflect light in a way that produces colour. These structures often give off metallic or iridescent colours that change as the light changes. The wings of the brilliant blue Ulysses Butterfly are covered in tiny scales that give off colour in this way.

Cicadas and others are coloured by pigments embedded in the cuticle. The colour appears the same no matter which angle the insect is viewed from. The Greengrocer Cicada (*Cyclochila australasiae*) is usually green, but may also be yellow, turquoise or pink. The colour is thought to be inherited and varies because the normal green is produced by a combination of yellow and turquoise. The colours of the Green Katydid (*Caedicia olivacea*) and other insects are influenced by the food eaten; when fed on a diet of red flower petals, katydids turn pink.

the FACTS!

SOME SPECIES of jewel beetle have special diffraction colours on their bodies that appear dull and colourless when in the shade (to hide them from predators) and brilliant in the sunlight (to attract mates).

TORTOISE BEETLES (*Charidotella sexpunctata*) can slowly change their colour from bright gold through green to brown over 20 minutes.

ADULT JEWEL beetles are so colourful that they have long been used for jewellery. Laws have been passed in some parts of the world to protect a number of species.

SOME INSECTS have patterns that can only be seen in ultraviolet light. The plain white wings of some butterflies, for example, may have ultraviolet patterns that can be seen by other insects but not by us.

BLUE DAMSELFLIES (*Austrolestes* spp.) may be bright blue during the day but become dull at dusk and continue to darken through the night. After sunrise, the characteristic blue returns.

MORE BRIGHT COLOURS are found on insects than on any other group of animals.

Left: A Jewel Bug. *Above:* Most longicorn beetles are a dull brown but there are a number of brightly coloured species.

WHY SO COLOURFUL?

The colours of insects (such as those on butterfly wings) are not there for our pleasure. Each has its own particular purpose, determined by the insect's needs and its way of life. Dark colours, for example, absorb heat when butterflies are basking in the sun in colder climates. Light colours reflect heat away from the body so that the butterflies do not overheat when flying around searching for nectar.

Warning colours are used to alert potential predators that the butterflies are poisonous (or else fool them into thinking so), while camouflage colours, such as mottled brown, are used to blend the butterflies against their background, particularly when at rest. Very bright colours are usually for the purposes of attracting a mate. These butterflies are more conspicuous to predators, but that is the risk they take in their efforts to reproduce.

Getting around
— locomotion without wings

Above: Looper caterpillars are missing legs in the middle of the body, which causes them to loop their bodies when travelling.

Getting around for most insects involves the use of legs. The juvenile stages of some insects, such as maggots, are legless, but the adult stage has the regular three pairs. Legs have been modified by various groups into an amazing range of shapes and functions. Some insects have also invented other ways of travel.

GETTING A LEG UP

The typical insect leg has five segments ending in a pair of claws to grip wet or rough surfaces, often coupled with a pad of sticky hairs for extra grip on slippery surfaces. Flies use such pads to enable them to climb glass and walk upside down on the ceiling. Water Striders have rows of water-repelling hairs at the ends of the legs that allow them to skate across water without sinking.

WHEN WALKING or running, each leg touches the ground in a well-defined order, which changes as speed increases or decreases. Recent studies suggest that when running at high speed, cockroaches may tuck up their front legs and run on their middle and hindlegs or even their hindlegs alone for short periods.

One way to travel quickly over short distances is by jumping. Grasshoppers, crickets, fleas and flea beetles jump using powerful hindlegs with very well developed muscles in the top half of the leg. The exoskeleton of the leg may also have hooks attached to other parts of the leg, storing energy that builds up and is released when the insect springs. The distance some insects travel in a single leap relative to their body length can be phenomenal.

Above: The body of this Hercules Moth caterpillar is lined with extremely strong suckers, called prolegs.

Left: The powerful hindlegs of grasshoppers and crickets enables them to leap considerable distances.

LIFE WITHOUT LEGS

Many insects live in confined areas where legs are useless. These insects move by contracting muscles inside the body so the front half is pushed forward and the rear is dragged up behind. Cup Moth caterpillars (*Doratifera vulnerans*, below) slide along leaf surfaces in a similar way.

the FACTS!

DRAGONFLY NYMPHS (below) move by tucking their legs in and forcing water out of the gill chamber in the end of the abdomen, streaking through the water with jet propulsion.

A FLEA'S JUMP is equivalent to a human jumping 250 m into the air. This would clear most high-rise buildings in Australian cities.

LARVAE OF DIVING BEETLES (*Acilius* spp.) are able to rapidly contract the muscles in the abdomen and shoot through the water, somersaulting as they go.

SOME INSECTS such as cockroaches and beetles are able to run at more than ten times the speed of a human relative to the number of body-lengths per second.

THE LARVAE of silken fungus beetles (*Antherophagus* spp.) sit on flowers and wait for bumblebees to visit, then grab onto the bee's legs to be transported to other flowers.

SOME INSECTS and related invertebrates move about by hitchhiking on other animals. This is known as "phoresy".

Life on the wing
— locomotion with wings

Apart from birds, bats and pterodactyls, only insects have developed active flight. This is undoubtedly one of the keys to their success. Flight probably began either when insects that were once aquatic used their gills to assist in gliding, or when terrestrial insects developed small lobes or flaps on the sides of their bodies.

IN BOTH CASES, even the smallest increase in the size of gills or flaps would make a falling insect much more stable and give them the tools to start gliding. Over many hundreds of generations, these lobes expanded and came under the insects' control, enabling them to switch from passive gliding to active flight.

Left: A female Orchard Butterfly in flight. Butterfly wings touch each other at the top and bottom of each stroke.

Right: Overlapping scales on the wing of a butterfly. There may be several hundred scales per millimetre.

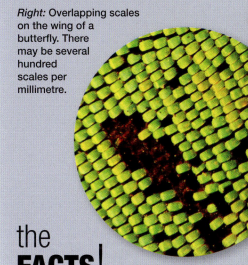

TWO PAIRS ARE BETTER THAN ONE

Apart from flies, almost all insects have two pairs of wings that may act independently of each other or work together. Dragonflies and lacewings, for example, are able to move each pair of wings separately, giving them the ability to manoeuvre in tight spaces. The forewings of moths are joined by a row of hooks to the hindwings so both pairs act in unison, enabling them to fly long distances. Dainty Swallowtails (*Papilio anactus*) use both pairs of wings when actively flying but only the hindwings when hovering to feed at flowers.

ADVANCED WINGS & LOST WINGS

Most insects are winged during the adult stage of the life cycle. Even fleas, in which all species are wingless, show signs of once having had wings but have lost them some time in the distant past. The wings of most insects are of a fairly basic design, geared towards keeping the insect in the air, sometimes for long periods. The wings of advanced fliers, such as dragonflies, are intricately constructed with complex systems of thin membranes (left), only a thousandth of a millimetre thick, working in conjunction with much thicker, reinforced sections.

The veins of the wings are able to bend and flatten to give strength at different parts of the wing stroke. This, together with the use of counterweights and other systems, enables insects to loop, roll, fly upside-down or turn at great speed. Many of the details of insect flight are still poorly understood.

the FACTS!

MOST OF THE ENERGY used in flight (93%) goes to keeping the insect in the air, while only a small proportion (7%) is used to propel the insect forward.

HUMANS HAVE NOT YET been able to design an artificial wing that comes close to what an insect wing can do.

THE ABILITY TO FLY is essential to many aspects of insect activity. Long distance migration and pollination, for example, both require insects to travel considerable distances in a relatively short time.

INSECTS HAVE BEEN FLYING for more than 300 million years and are still by far the most numerous group of flying animals on Earth.

THE WINGS of some winged insects are too small and slow to work effectively. They rely heavily on the wind to get airborne.

THE SLOWEST FLIERS are the butterflies, whose wings move at about ten wingbeats per second. Mosquitoes can flap their wings at more than 600 beats per second.

THE FLIGHT muscles of insects must reach a certain temperature before they can operate properly.

Living under water
— aquatic insects

Above: Toad Bugs live on the edges of ponds. Adults are predatory and leap onto their prey.

Right: A Dragonfly nymph.

Centre: A dragonfly emerging from its nymphal skin after crawling from a pond at night.

the FACTS!

WATER BEETLES can stay under water for long periods by taking a bubble of air from the surface and carrying it around with them, using it to breathe.

THE LARVAE of a type of beetle called a Water Penny (*Psephenus* sp.) have suckers on the underside of the body. These suckers are so strong that they are able to hold on to rocks in the strongest of waterfalls.

ADULT SPERCHEID beetles spend their lives walking around upside down on the underside of the surface film of stagnant ponds.

SOME INSECTS live in very specific habitats. Hydraenid beetles (*Tympanogaster* sp.) live only in the narrow band of rock at the edge of streams where they are not covered by water but are kept wet by the splashes.

ALL MAYFLIES, stoneflies, dragonflies, damselflies, alderflies and caddisflies have aquatic nymphs and larvae.

Many different types of insects have taken to living a freshwater life in Australia. They also share the streams and ponds with other invertebrate groups such as crustaceans, leeches, spiders, molluscs and even sponges and jellyfish. Freshwater insects make up about 3% of all insect species.

FROM SEEP TO SEA

Australia is the driest inhabited continent and has comparatively little runoff into streams and rivers; however, waterways in many areas are teeming with life. Which insects live where depends in part on the type of waterway. Many waterways often begin with a spring or "seep" where semi-aquatic insects such as toad bugs can disperse or burrow into the ground if the spring dries up.

Other insects, such as water beetle larvae, appear as the spring flows into a stream. In fast-flowing streams, the insects living on the bottom (such as Water Pennies) may be so flat that the rushing water has no effect on them and they can move about freely. Other insects (such as midge larvae) are equipped with a row of suckers to help them hang on. In ponds and other slow-flowing waterways, fly larvae and water bugs can move up and down through the water column without being swept away. As streams merge into large rivers and eventually flow into the sea, the insect population gradually changes and finally disappears altogether.

THEIR PLACE IN THE COLUMN

In any patch of water, insect populations are divided by their position in the water column. Whirligig beetles, Water Scorpions (*Laccotrephes tristis*), water striders and backswimmers move around on and just under the water surface, feeding on terrestrial insects that have fallen in and become trapped. Moving through open water are creeping water bugs, diving beetles and water boatmen. The legs of many species are lined with long thick hairs that act as oars as the insect paddles through the water. On the bottom of the waterway, the nymphs and larvae of dragonflies, damselflies, mayflies, stoneflies and caddisflies patrol, feeding on organic matter, aquatic plants or each other.

Building a home
— insect shelters

To protect themselves from predators, parasites and bad weather, many insects build shelters or hide in burrows. Burrows are dug in the ground or under stones for shelter, but tunnels in leaves, seeds or tree trunks are usually excavated as part of the insects' search for food.

Above: Case moth caterpillars enlarge the case as they grow. This caterpillar is using silk to attach new twigs.

MOTHS THAT PUPATE in an exposed situation such as among leaves or on a tree trunk, spin a silken cocoon around themselves for protection. Fragments of leaf litter or bark may be incorporated into the silk to camouflage the cocoon, or prickly hairs from the caterpillar may be pushed through the cocoon as a further defence. Moths that pupate in sheltered situations, such as under bark or in soil, do not generally spin a cocoon. The Saunder's Case Moth caterpillar (*Oiketicus elongatus*) weaves a silken bag that is covered in sticks to camouflage and protect itself. Although extremely tough, the bag can be torn open by persistent birds.

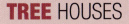

Left: There are more than 350 species of case moth in Australia, each using slightly different materials to build its case.

the FACTS!

DESPITE INSECTS being such superb builders, insect shelters do not protect the majority of them from predators and parasites.

LERP INSECTS spin a protective covering with sugary substances exuded from the mouth. These coverings, called lerps, may be highly decorative and are unique to each species.

POTTER WASPS construct intricate nests of mud and clay in which they deposit their eggs. Before sealing the nest, the female provisions it with sufficient food to last the larva until adulthood.

ANTLIONS DIG small pits in sand in which they wait patiently. Passing ants tumble into the pits and are quickly eaten.

TERMITES LIVING in rainforests may build a stack of umbrella-shaped structures over the top of the mound to keep off the heavy rain.

TREE HOUSES

Tree-dwelling ants such as Green Tree Ants (*Oecophylla smaragdina*, right) use silk from the larvae to sew together leaves, forming an effective, well-defended shelter. Ants leave the nest to collect food and patrol the surrounding foliage and at night they may set up highways to transfer larvae between nests. A single colony of ants may include dozens of individual nests, spread between a number of nearby trees.

SUN WORSHIPPERS

Perhaps the biggest and most complex shelters are constructed by termites. Mounds are built to draw air and circulate it through a series of connected chambers, heating or cooling the mound depending on the location and the circumstances. The Magnetic Termites (*Amitermes meridionalis*) of the Northern Territory build massive structures more than 2 m high. Despite their common name, the termites do not orient their mounds towards magnetic north, but do take advantage of the morning sun. The eastern face of the mound is rapidly heated in the morning so termite activity can begin early in the day. In the afternoon this face is shaded and remains fairly cool.

Living in groups
— social insects

Above: Green Tree Ants work cooperatively to carry a Glasswing Butterfly pupa.

Many insects demonstrate early signs of social behaviour. These "subsocial" behaviours may be as simple as raising the young cooperatively, or moving about and feeding as a group.

the FACTS!

BECAUSE OF THEIR LARGE numbers, honeybees can stay warm during winter by clustering around the queen and vibrating their wings to generate heat.

SOCIAL INSECTS such as honeybees are the only insects known to have a complex language. They "dance" within the hive to let other workers know the exact location of groups of flowers or other resources.

SOME ANT and bee colonies grow by "budding" — dividing an existing nest into two smaller colonies, which then go on to grow and mature themselves.

INSECT SOCIETIES are maintained by chemical communication between their members. Workers recognise each other by smell and the queen uses hormones to regulate the growth and behaviour of the workers.

LARGE INSECT SOCIETIES may have a considerable impact on their surrounding environments. Nutrient recycling and prey collection by millions of ants or termites from a single nest can influence other plants and animals over a wide area.

MALES TEND to be rare in insect societies. They are usually produced only for a short time during spring and may die straight after mating.

A NUMBER OF AUSTRALIAN cockroach species and passalid beetles protect and feed their young until they are old enough to fend for themselves. Steelblue Sawfly larvae (*Perga* sp.) shelter as a group during the day and move about to feed at night, following a single leader and communicating with each other as they travel.

Above: Passalid beetles live communally in family groups under logs; this is probably the first step towards sociality.

A BRIGHT FOUR CASTE

Truly social insects are found among the ants, bees, wasps and termites, which have been operating as societies for many millions of years. Social insects are defined by a number of generations living together in a single nest, cooperatively raising young that are not necessarily their own.

A group of social insects may have up to four "castes", where labour is divided between different groups of insects within the same nest. Castes may include "reproductives", such as the king and queen termites, major workers (which leave the nest to forage), minor workers (which do not) and guards (which defend the nest from intruders). The workers of European Honey Bees (*Apis mellifera*) undertake different tasks throughout their lives, such as nursing, guarding and foraging, changing jobs as they age.

Left: Termites form the largest societies in the world.

Right: A group of related paper wasps constructing a nest. Small white eggs can be seen in the cells.

THE BIG FOUR

Termite colonies are founded by a single pair of termites, the king and queen, which begin to construct a nest. The abdomen of the queen begins to swell as she develops eggs and she may go on to produce many millions of young throughout her life. As workers are produced (below) they begin to expand the nest, collect food and defend the colony. Working cooperatively, a termite colony is far more efficient and successful than individual termites could be working on their own.

The more advanced wasps, bees and ants have an extra level of defence, as most species are able to sting intruders that may threaten the nest. Unlike termites, the adults of these groups feed on different foods from their young, which enables them to make more use of the available resources. Adults collect carbohydrates such as nectar for themselves and proteins such as meat or dead insects for the growing larvae.

Living with others — mutualism

Above: Treehoppers with their protectors, Green Tree Ants.

Many insect species have improved their survival rate and ability to secure food by working cooperatively with other insect (or even vertebrate or plant) species. Such cooperative behaviour between different species is known as "mutualism".

WELCOME HOUSE GUESTS

A number of different types of beetles and other insects may live inside the nests of termites, ants or bees. These insects are known as "inquilines". They are generally tolerated by their hosts and may even be protected and fed by the hosts, in exchange for a reward. Many inquilines possess special glands or tufts of hair on their bodies that produce a substance attractive as food for the hosts. Several types of Australian specialist beetles have a body shape almost indistinguishable from that of termites and are groomed and treated by the termites as one of their own.

the FACTS!

AMBROSIA BEETLES carry around microscopic organisms in pockets on their bodies. These organisms help the beetles break down and digest the dead wood on which they feed.

ONE OF THE MOST COMMON forms of mutualism is between ants and sap-sucking bugs such as aphids. The ants protect the bugs in return for honeydew produced as a by-product of the bugs' feeding.

THE CATERPILLAR of the Common Imperial Blue butterfly (*Jalmenus evagoras*) produces a sweet substance from an organ on its back. Ants feed on the organ in return for providing protection from predators and parasites.

THE SUGAR IN HONEYDEW is not derived only from plants. About one third of its sugars comes from the blood sugar of the insects that produce it.

Left: Lycaenid caterpillars, often attended by ants, produce a sweet liquid laced with pheromones.

Above: Eurymelid bugs produce a sweet honeydew as a by-product of their feeding. Ants feed on this honeydew.

TREE HOUSES FOR ANTS

In certain cases insects such as ants will guard a tree or bush against plant-eating insects in return for nectar produced by special glands in the plants' stems. The Queensland Ant Plant has a swollen base filled with connecting chambers which houses and provides nectar for an entire ant nest. The ants, usually a type of meat ant (*Iridomyrmex cordatus*), in turn keep other insects from devouring the leaves and the plant also gains nutrients from the ants' waste. This enables the plant to live in areas where it otherwise could not because essential nutrients are not available. Insects also have a long and literally fruitful association with plants, particularly through the process of pollination.

SOWING THE SEEDS

Many native plant seeds have nutritious appendages (elaiosomes) that are attractive to ants. The ants take the inedible seeds into the nest 80 m or more away from the tree and consume the elaiosome, leaving the seed to germinate underground. The elaiosomes may contain, as well as nutrients, chemical compounds that alter the ants' behaviour and make seed dispersal more rapid. Fifteen hundred species of Australian plants produce seeds with elaiosomes, compared to 300 species in the rest of the world.

Below: Scale insects produce honeydew for a range of ant species. The ants may worsen the problems caused by scale pests.

Eating plants
— herbivory

Above: Caterpillars often feed at night to avoid daytime predators. Most species have a characteristic chewing pattern.

Because the great majority of insects are plant eaters, they have a substantial impact on the Australian flora. Although some plant species are insect-free, most are attacked to some degree, but overall feeding is at a low level and the populations generally remain in balance.

MANY CATERPILLARS feed by skeletonising the leaves, taking off the top layer of green (left), leaving behind the veins.

FIGHTING BACK

In response to this onslaught, plants defend themselves in a number of ways. Mechanical means include tough leaves with waxy or slippery surfaces, sharp spines and sticky hairs that injure or trap insects or wear down their mouthparts. Some plants are able to starve insects of essential nutrients such as nitrogen. The majority of plants protect themselves using chemicals, often in conjunction with mechanical defences. These chemicals are a complex and varied group of compounds that serve to deter, repel, sterilise or kill the insects, or, more subtly, to slow down insect growth.

ANY PLANT may be attacked by insects in a variety of ways. Beetles chew the leaves while moth caterpillars tunnel through the inside of the leaf, leaving the outer part intact and destroying the insides. Bugs suck sap, causing new shoots to wilt and die. Moth and beetle larvae bore through the trunks and stems while tiny flies form galls on the branches. Root feeders can cause significant damage underground while a range of insects chew the flowers, seeds and fruits. Plants can often cope with individual attacks but may succumb if a number of attacks occur together.

the FACTS!

THERE ARE MORE SPECIES of insects in the world that eat green plants than there are species of green plants.

IT HAS BEEN estimated that up to half the foliage in a eucalypt forest is removed each year by insects.

UNDER CERTAIN circumstances plagues of insects may arise and destroy whole forests. In 1957 the Gumleaf Skeletoniser (*Uraba lugens*) stripped gum trees of leaves over 40,000 ha in Victoria.

IN SOME areas, up to 70% of the leaves produced by a gum tree each year are consumed by insects — possibly the greatest insect attack on any tree in the world.

AUSTRALIAN GUM TREES grown in other parts of the world proliferate without their heavy burden of plant-eating insects. Consequently, some gum tree species have become major weeds overseas.

THE VERY PRESENCE of insects may have a detrimental effect on plants. The dung dropped by insects feeding on gum trees has chemicals in it that may suppress germination and growth of the seedlings below.

Above: Although small, leaf beetles have had a dramatic effect on the evolution of their hosts — Australian gum trees.

Below: Very young caterpillars rarely damage plants, but as they grow their feeding can cause serious problems.

Above: Stick insects are generally uncommon, but occasionally plagues can occur; entire forests of gum trees can be defoliated.

THE COUNTER-ATTACK

Some plants produce a thick, sticky sap that clogs up an insect's mouthparts. In response, the insect will cut the main vein of the leaf to drain out the sap before feeding. Other insects can neutralise toxic compounds by combining them into a harmless chemical, breaking them down, or by adding their own chemicals to counteract the toxins' effects. Insects such as the toxic Wanderer Butterfly (*Danaus plexippus*) absorb the plants' chemical defences and use them as their own.

Making more plants
— pollination

Plants produce flowers as the first step in making more plants. They need to receive pollen from other flowers of the same species in order for fertilisation to occur. To help this happen, flowers supply nectar that is attractive to insects and the insects carry pollen from one flower to another on their feeding routes. Pollination of flowers by insects began when flowering plants first evolved and has been perfected over the last 130 million years.

Above: A female Cairns Birdwing Butterfly covered in pollen. Plants produce millions of times more pollen than is required to reproduce.

Bottom: Plants that produce mass blooms attract large numbers of pollinators, including beetles.

THE FLOWERS' GAMBLE

The flowers of some species are designed to attract all insects, with big showy petals and a sweet smell. In fact, the sole purpose of most flowers is to attract insects. The petals bear dark ultraviolet patterns that direct insects to the nectar at the base and some flowers have a runway to make landing easier!

These flowers are visited by beetles, flies, moths, butterflies, native bees and wasps, but the chances of any one of those insects then visiting another flower of the same species is fairly low. Other flowers are designed to be visited by only one local insect species and, although they are visited less often, the chance of fertilisation is high. Some orchid species in Western Australia have petals that mimic the shape and colour of certain native wasp females, and are only visited by male wasps that try to mate with them.

the FACTS!

SOME PLANTS have a pressure-sensitive platform as part of the flower. When a pollinator lands, the mechanism is tripped and a packet of pollen is thrust onto the insect's abdomen by the flower's stigma.

MORE THAN ONE THIRD of all the world's food crops are pollinated by insects and many other agricultural products, such as beef, rely on pollinators to fertilise pasture.

SOME PLANT SPECIES package their pollen into small parcels called "pollinia". These are deposited by the flower on the backs of visiting insects.

IN ARID AREAS OF AUSTRALIA, some bee species fly at night to take advantage of the short flowering time of desert plants in response to rainfall.

THE VALUE of insect pollinators to the world's food producers has been estimated at nearly $200 billion p.a.

Top: Butterflies will pollinate a range of plants, but prefer large blooms of deep-throated flowers.

Above: A long, thin longicorn beetle feeding on the pollen of a native bottlebrush.

DESIGNED FOR THE TASK

Many insects are specifically designed to feed on flowers and to promote pollination. The mouthparts of butterflies are modified into a long tube called a proboscis, which is designed to draw nectar up from deep flowers. Many types of bees carry pollen in a basket-like arrangement of hairs on their back legs and tend to visit the flowers of one plant species on each collecting trip, thereby ensuring fertilisation of that species. This habit gives the honey of European Honey Bees the flavour of the dominant plant species around the hive.

Attack
— predatory insects

Above: A spider wasp taking a spider into its hole.

Below: An assassin bug feeding on a ladybird.

Only about 5% of all insects are predatory, so in any community, predators are much scarcer than their prey and rarely have much effect on the prey population. All members of groups such as dragonflies and mantids are predatory, while others such as stick insects have no predatory members.

STUDIES SHOW that although predators are apparently perfectly adapted for capturing prey, they often have a low success rate. However, defence is very important in insect prey populations because a large proportion of those born are eaten before reaching maturity.

DAVID VS GOLIATH

Most predatory insects prey on other insects smaller than themselves, but some groups (such as mantids and water scorpions) will take fish, frogs and even birds several times larger than themselves. Many predators cut prey into pieces and eat whole chunks; others such as assassin bugs pierce the prey with their proboscis and suck out the juices. Green Lacewing larvae (*Chrysoperla* sp.) have a pair of long, curved mandibles that are pointed and hollow. The larvae use these mandibles to pierce prey and suck them dry, then carry around the empty husks on their backs as camouflage.

Right: These tiny ants are able to overcome a much larger assassin bug because it is at its most vulnerable while moulting.

the FACTS!

LARVAE OF *BRACHYPSECTRA* spp. beetles lie motionless and wait for small spiders to pass by. The spiders are impaled with a sudden movement of a spine at the end of the larva's abdomen.

ADULT PAUSSID BEETLES have a pair of thick, flat antennae that ooze a sweet substance which is irresistible to ants. The beetle eats any ants that come close.

A SINGLE LADYBIRD larva may eat up to 100 aphids per day.

ADULTS OF THE BEETLE called the Devil's Coach-horse (*Creophilus* sp.) perch on dead carcasses. They capture blowflies attracted to the carcass to lay eggs, then tear open the flies' abdomens and consume the eggs inside.

STEP ONE — FIND FOOD

Obtaining food is more difficult for predators than for plant-eating insects, so predators have developed a range of strategies to firstly find food and secondly capture it. Most predators will feed on a range of prey and, like vertebrate predators, tend to go for the slower and weaker animals that are easier to catch.

A predator may begin searching randomly, then narrow its search and refine its behaviour as it enters a habitat where prey is most likely to be, or when it perceives the presence of nearby prey. A ladybird larva that feeds on aphids will stop frequently as it searches and swing its head from side to side. This goes on until the larva contacts and consumes an aphid, then it concentrates its searching pattern once it resumes hunting, as other aphids are likely to be found near the first victim.

While some predators feed on sedentary prey such as scale insects, most have to seek, chase and overpower the prey before it can be consumed. Predators need good eyesight and the ability to move rapidly. Dragonflies, damselflies and robber flies are the only insects able to catch prey on the wing. Other insects are ambush predators, waiting patiently for hours on end for prey to pass within reach.

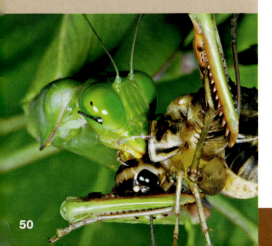

Left: A Giant Mantid easily slices through the body of a cricket with its powerful mandibles.

MASSIVE ATTACK

Social insects are able to subdue prey many times larger than themselves by cooperatively pinning down and dismembering large prey. Although stingless, Green Tree Ants (*Oecophylla smaragdina*, left) are able to do this by calling in large numbers of workers to help, but ants such as bull ants are able to individually overpower prey with their powerful stings. Paper wasps dismember their prey on the spot so only the most useful parts of the prey need to be carried back to the nest. Other solitary wasps paralyse prey with their stings before carrying their victims back to the nest alive and fresh.

Above: Due to their large size, bull ants are often able to carry prey items too big for other ant species.

ON THE ATTACK

Predatory insects use an array of attack mechanisms to make prey capture easier. The eyes of praying mantids are large and powerful, situated on a small mobile head that allows 360° vision. Their forelegs are lightning fast and lined with sharp spines to hold prey once caught. Mantispid lacewings and water scorpions, though unrelated, have similarly spined and powerful front legs.

Feather-legged Assassin Bugs (*Ptilocnemus femoralis*) feed on aggressive Jumping Jacks (*Myrmecia* sp.) ants. The bugs secrete a chemical that subdues the ants so the bugs can feed on them unharmed. Other assassin bugs smear their legs with tree sap that attracts small insect prey and traps them. Ants, bees and wasps are usually armed with a powerful sting that can paralyse or kill prey within seconds. Dragonfly nymphs have an extendible pair of jaws under their heads that shoot out to grasp passing prey.

the FACTS!

WITHOUT PREDATORS, many insect populations would spiral out of control. A single housefly, without any controls whatsoever, may eventually produce 20 million flies within a single summer.

SPIDERS ARE NOT THE ONLY predators that capture prey with silk. Caddisflies and fungus midges also spin snares to trap other insects.

CANNIBALISM is very common among insects. Many species will consume unrelated members of the same species, as well as their brothers and sisters and even their own offspring.

PREDATORY INSECTS are useful in controlling insect pests, not just in the backyard, but also for large scale control of introduced species.

MANY INSECT groups that are not known for their predatory behaviour, such as butterflies and moths, contain a few members that do feed opportunistically on insect prey.

MANY TYPES OF BEETLES are predatory. Tiger beetles are among the fastest of insects, running at up to 600 mm per second in pursuit of their prey.

MOST INSECTS have biting mandibles rather than sucking or piercing mouthparts. The two mandibles move against each other like a pair of sliding doors and can cut through the toughest prey.

PREDATORY INSECTS have been recorded feeding on a range of vertebrates. These include fish, lizards, small birds and even mice.

Left: The Feather-legged Assassin Bug feeds exclusively on jumping ants.

Protecting themselves
— defence mechanisms

Insects defend themselves against predators with a range of ingenious adaptations. The most common method is to rapidly leave the scene, by running or flying away, or dropping off a branch and feigning death.

MORE AGGRESSIVE defensive strategies may be so effective that the prey can in fact kill the predator, so predators have developed strategies to protect themselves from intended victims.

Above: Paper wasps are always ready to defend the nest and will fly out in a group at the slightest disturbance.

Right: Bull ants are equipped for both defence and attack, with a pair of powerful mandibles at the front and a painful sting at the rear.

Top: The stinging spines of the Mottled Cup Moth can be retracted when danger has passed.

Right: Earwigs possess a large pair of pincers at the end of the abdomen. The pincers are waved as a warning at any approaching threat.

CHEMICAL WARFARE

Many insects secrete an offensive substance that may poison or repel attackers. Bombardier Beetles (*Pheropsophus verticalis*) release an explosive charge of hydrogen peroxide that leaves the beetle's abdomen at boiling point and stuns or kills the predator.

The Bronze Orange Bug (*Musgraveia sulciventris*) lives on citrus trees and can squirt an evil-smelling, highly irritating substance into the eyes.

Swallowtail caterpillars, such as the Orchard Butterfly (*Papilio aegeus*), have an osmeterium just behind the head. This is a red or orange fleshy organ that is normally kept inside the body but suddenly appears when the caterpillar is attacked. It produces a rotting citrus smell.

Right: The Spiny Leaf Beetle (*Hispellinus* sp.) is covered with spines which may serve as protection against predators.

the FACTS!

WHEN DISTURBED, byrrhid beetles can retract their legs and other appendages into special cavities around the body (in a similar fashion to tortoises).

WHEN TIPPED ONTO THEIR backs, click beetles have a flipping mechanism that throws them up into the air. Three quarters of the time they will land on their feet and quickly escape.

DARKLING BEETLES (*Eurychora* sp.) live in deserts and have special structures on their backs that hold sand. When threatened, they stop moving and blend in with the surrounding sand.

ADULT TENEBRIONID BEETLES (*Encara floccosum*) live among moss and lichen-covered rocks. Their bodies are covered with long white structures that hide them perfectly in their environment.

AN EFFECTIVE COMBINATION

Insects such as Prickly Katydids (*Phricta spinosa*) adopt a number of defensive strategies. They are superbly camouflaged, heavily armoured and covered with prickly spines. These katydids are also equipped with powerful legs to kick out at an attacker and bright red patches on the insides of the hindlegs that they flash when disturbed.

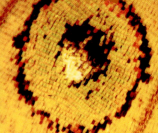

Above, left to right: When disturbed, this arctiid moth produces an orange frothy fluid from glands in the thorax, accompanied by a sizzling sound; Detail of a small eyespot on the wing of a Cruiser Butterfly — some predators may mistake this for a genuine eye; This fleshy red organ, called an osmeterium, suddenly appears from behind the head of a Cairns Birdwing Butterfly caterpillar when it is threatened.

BATTLING THE BIRDS

Many birds specialise in feeding on insects. Birds are visual predators and they search using images based on the outline of insects imprinted on their brains through experience. Insects that are able to change or conceal their outline are more likely to avoid being eaten. They do this through camouflage and with obscure body shapes that are difficult to detect. With the search image set, birds can be easily startled by the sudden appearance of something new. Consequently, many insects give a "startle display" when disturbed. Female Goliath Stick Insects (*Eurycnema goliath*) are camouflaged light green, but when the camouflage fails they suddenly lift their wings to reveal a striking crimson flash underneath.

Above: Prickly caterpillars, such as the White Stemmed Gum Moth (*Chelepteryx collesi*), push their spines through the wall of their cocoons to protect them when they pupate.

DISPOSABLE BODY PARTS

Many insects are designed to lose a certain part of their bodies in an emergency, providing valuable time to escape during an attack. When approached by a predatory ladybird larva, an aphid may kick out at its attacker, often losing its leg but retaining its life. Mayfly nymphs have a pair of long cerci at the end of the abdomen, which help signal the approach of a predatory stonefly nymph. If attacked from behind, the mayfly may lose one of its cerci, but escape otherwise unharmed.

Some well-camouflaged moth species have a pair of large eyespots on their hindwings (like the Emperor Gum Moth below), usually black within a ring of blue or green. The eyespots are normally hidden away under the forewings, but are suddenly exposed by the moth when disturbed. To a visual predator such as a bird, a pair of owl-like eyes suddenly looking back at it may cause enough hesitation for the moth to escape.

Some insects have false eyes or a false head to divert a predator's attack away from its real head. Birds in particular attack insects by first going for the head. Many types of butterflies, such as the Common Brown (*Heteronympha merope*) and Cruiser (*Vindula arsinoe*) have a number of small eyespots along the outer edges of the wings. Others, such as the Common Imperial Blue (*Jalmenus evagoras*), have a false head and body — complete with false legs and antennae — at the tail end of the wings. If a bird attacks the false head, the butterfly takes off in the opposite direction, with just a small piece of wing missing.

the FACTS!

BOMBARDIER BEETLES (*Brachynus* spp.) use chemicals from inside the body to produce loud explosions from the end of the abdomen when disturbed. The chemicals produce a boiling hot mixture at about 100°C that can create up to 20 explosions per minute.

WHEN DISTURBED, the beetle called Spanish Fly (*Lytta vesicatoria*) can produce a chemical called cantharidin, which is fatal to humans even in very small doses.

THE GREAT WATER BEETLE (*Dytiscus* sp.), when disturbed, gives off a milky substance that quickly puts fish into a deep sleep.

MANY CATERPILLARS sport spines and stinging hairs; others secrete wax that clogs up the predator's mouthparts; others cover themselves with heavy body armour.

THE GREEN MANTID (*Orthodera ministralis*) has a blue eyespot on the inside of each foreleg. It flashes these when cornered.

TORTOISE BEETLES (*Aspidomorpha* spp.) protect themselves with shields of their own dried dung. The shield is held over the body at all times.

Getting the message across
— communication

Insects use communication for various reasons — to avoid predators (warning colours), to defend a territory (calling) or to lure prey to their deaths (chemical attractants). The messages communicated are varied and may include bluffing and false messages in order to deceive opponents in contests. However, the main purpose of communication between insects is to attract a mate.

the FACTS!

THE GIANT Burrowing Cockroach (*Macropanesthia rhinoceros*) expels air from its body when disturbed; this produces a hissing noise.

SOCIAL INSECTS (such as ants) tap each other's antennae to determine whether they are members of the same nest. They use chemical communication (such as pheromones) as a back-up to their system of touch.

MALE MOLE CRICKETS (*Gryllotalpa* spp.) use the architecture of their singing burrows to produce one of the loudest insect songs in the world (second only to some cicada species). The song produced by using the burrows as amplifiers is up to 200 times louder than the same song produced at the soil's surface.

DEATH-WATCH BEETLES in Europe live inside timber. They communicate with each other by knocking their heads on the wood in a rapid series of taps.

DRAGONFLIES AND damselflies are often territorial throughout their lives. The aquatic nymphs "posture" to keep other nymphs out of their territories. Posturing includes raising their bodies off the stream bottom and waving their abdomens aggressively.

JOIN IN THE CHORUS

Thousands of insect species produce sound in one way or another. Male cicadas use song to attract females — two plates under the abdomen (tymbals) vibrate to produce sound. Vibrations at speeds up to 36,000 per second merge together to create the characteristic cicada song. The abdomen is almost hollow to amplify the sound and a muscle attached to the tymbal increases its volume. The cicada also uses muscles to expand and bend the abdomen, which changes the song pattern. A group of male Greengrocer Cicadas (*Cyclochila australasiae*) generate sound louder than a jet engine; enough to break local councils' noise regulations.

Above: Cicadas are the best known singers in the insect world. This Bladder Cicada has an enlarged abdomen to amplify the sound.

Above: A female Orchard Butterfly is surrounded by males, each showering her in a cloud of pheromones.

LIVING VIOLINS

Insects such as crickets, bugs and beetles produce sound by scraping one part of the body across another and emitting a rasping, squeaking or grinding sound, generally used to startle predators. This is known as "stridulation". One part of the body possesses a comb-like file and another part a scraper — a pointed appendage that is drawn over the file. Crickets have a file and scraper on opposing wings and rub these together to produce their familiar chirping.

Below: Mole crickets live in trumpet-shaped underground burrows that amplify their song.

LOOK AT ME

Communication is often visual. Fireflies (left) are able to produce light from the underside of their abdomens to attract mates after dark. Light is generated by combining a chemical called luciferin with oxygen, and brightness is controlled by the beetle's air intake. The pattern of flashing is generally unique to each species so that males can locate suitable females.

Living in Australia
— adapting to extremes

Insects play an essential role in the ecology of all Australian environments. They form the basis of most terrestrial and freshwater food chains and are the staple diet of some plant species; all spiders; most centipedes, scorpions, freshwater fish, frogs, reptiles and birds; and many mammals.

A LONG HISTORY

Present Australian insect populations have been determined to a large extent by climate. In the distant past, Australia was located much further south on our planet, as part of the supercontinent Gondwana. As Australia moved slowly northwards it passed through different climate zones and underwent extensive mountain building and erosion, and inundation by glaciers and inland seas, as well as periods of warming and cooling. All this while, insect groups evolved and radiated across Australia — or retreated to become extinct as climates, floras and faunas changed.

Above: Australia has thousands of tiny streams, home to a great variety of mayfly species.

Below, left: Cockroaches abound in Australia's deserts, living under tree bark or in sandy burrows.

Above: This member of the unlikely-looking pie-dish beetle group lives in desert regions and has wide flanges surrounding the entire body.

the FACTS!

TO SURVIVE IN HARSH environments, many insect species are able to withstand desiccation to their bodies during times of crisis (to the point where they are as close to death as is biologically possible).

ALTHOUGH INSECTS are able to survive in salt water, there are very few species that have colonised the ocean. This is probably because all the niches have been taken by crustaceans, which were there long before insects evolved.

EACH YEAR thousands of insects leave Australian shores and are carried hundreds of kilometres across oceans by strong winds. Most perish on the journey, but a few manage to colonise small islands or even other continents.

SOME INSECTS, such as Australian Plague Locusts (*Chortoicetes terminifera*) escape extreme environments by migrating away. Locust migrations may comprise many millions of individuals.

DESERT ANTS (*Ocymyrmex* spp.) living in the Namib Desert in Africa venture out during the day to feed on insects killed by the heat. They can survive temperatures higher than 60°C.

ESCAPING THE HEAT

By far the largest habitat in Australia is desert, which covers two-thirds of the continent. Desert is an extremely variable habitat, including vast stony plains, claypans, sand dunes and mountain ranges. The desert is a very harsh environment with temperatures up to 53°C during the day and below freezing at night. Food is scarce and insect activity is generally restricted to the evening and night, but insects are nevertheless plentiful. The most common insects in Australian deserts are ants (including the well-known honeypot ants) termites and beetles, all well adapted to desert life.

LIVING WITH US

Australia has a remarkable range of habitats, from eucalypt woodlands to rainforests, and from grasslands to alpine snowfields. The human environment includes our houses, gardens, parks, rubbish tips, orchards, crop lands and pastures. This is the largest habitat in Australia after deserts and more than half of the country has been modified by people. Many native insects have entered this habitat, but it is dominated by introduced species. A few native species, such as Christmas beetles (*Anoplognathus* spp.), Black Field Crickets (*Teleogryllus commodus*) and Orchard Butterflies (*Papilio aegeus*) are able to survive and have even increased in number in this new habitat.

Insects' enemies
— natural foes of insects

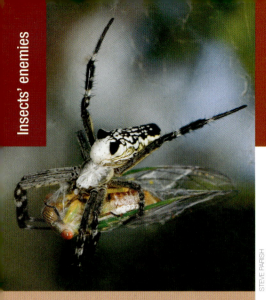

Above: Large insects such as cicadas are too big for many predators but can be successfully captured in strong webs.

Because there are so many insects available as food, they have many natural enemies. These foes can be divided into predators, parasites and diseases. Worldwide there are also more than 500 plant species that consume insects; these plants are found anywhere from deserts to snowfields, but are most common in rainforests.

A NUMBER of invertebrates such as scorpions, centipedes and pseudoscorpions feed on insects. Spiders, with their ingenious array of traps and snares to capture flying insects, are their most important predators. Entire families of spiders have developed specific adaptations (such as net casting or leaping from great distances) to ambush insects.

VERTEBRATES VS INVERTEBRATES

Most mammals consume insects in at least some part of their diet. Small marsupials, rodents and bats feed almost exclusively on insects. Because of the abundance of insects in Australia, there is a greater abundance of insect-eating mammals, birds and reptiles than in other parts of the world. Even meat-eating mammals (including the introduced fox and cat) eat insects as a major component of their diet. Plant and nectar feeding mammals and birds must also catch insects on occasion to gain essential protein and nutrients.

The greatest insect-eating vertebrates are birds, expert at catching insects on the wing and often moving vast distances to follow swarms. Frogs and small reptiles feed almost exclusively on insects, and may have an effect on ground-dwelling insect populations.

Above: A small bug has been trapped by the sticky head of a sundew, a plant that feeds on insects.

INSECT ILLNESS

One of the greatest groups of natural insect enemies are pathogens. These include viruses, bacteria, fungi and protozoa and they often cause insect diseases. European Honey Bees (*Apis mellifera*), for example, are attacked by viruses, while bacteria (such as foulbrood and honeybee paralysis), sometimes cause hives to die out altogether. Insects can be attacked by fungi that take over the entire body and send out fruiting bodies that produce millions of spores to infect other insects.

Above: This caterpillar has been attacked by a virus that breaks down all the cells in the body, leaving only a bag of fluid.

the FACTS!

MANY TYPES of viruses and fungi are used by scientists to control insect pests. These spread very effectively and may also be specific to particular pest species.

SOME INSECTS hang around carnivorous plants, feeding on other insects trapped by the plant.

ECHIDNAS AND NUMBATS feed almost exclusively on ants and termites. Thorny Devils do the same, sitting patiently along ant trails and collecting workers with their sticky tongues.

FORK-TAILED SWIFTS move from Asia into northern Australia each year to feed on migrating insects. These birds feed on the wing and never land on Australian soil.

BATS FIND insects in flight using echolocation. Some moths, lacewings and crickets are able to evade bats by dropping to the ground when they hear the echolocating clicks from the bats.

BUSH FLY (*Musca vetustissima*) populations are controlled to some extent by the fungus *Entomophthora muscae*. After killing the fly, the fungus starts to protrude through its skin and releases a mass of spores to the wind.

Big & small
— insect size

There are many advantages to being small. Many insects are able to survive on relatively small resources (a single tree or even an individual leaf). Parasitic insects can spend their entire lives within the body of a single caterpillar (or even a single insect egg). Being small also helps insects hide from predators.

Above: The Giant Burrowing Cockroach is Australia's largest cockroach and one of the heaviest in the world.

Left: Sitting on one of these katydid eggs is a tiny wasp about to lay its own eggs. Parasitic wasps tend to be very, very small.

AIR FACTOR

The biggest insects now living on Earth are significantly smaller than many of the prehistoric insects. One of the main reasons is their breathing system. Insects breathe through holes in their sides, called spiracles, which transport oxygen through tracheae to every cell in the body. In the early stages of insect evolution, oxygen levels on Earth were higher than they are now, allowing oxygen to be transferred more efficiently. At the current lower levels, very big insects find it difficult to gain enough oxygen to remain active.

For the same reason, the largest insects alive today tend to be found in tropical areas. Not only does increased temperature and humidity enable them to grow and remain active throughout the year, these same conditions enhance oxygen transfer through the spiracles and tracheae.

Above: There are many large grasshoppers in Australia but this species, appropriately called the Giant Grasshopper (*Valanga irregularis*), is the largest.

MICRO MOTHS

The average insect is less than ten millimetres long, but some predatory insects need to be big in order to overcome their prey. However, predators are relatively uncommon in the insect world and it is a less successful way of life than eating plants. More than half the world's insects are plant eaters and most of these are particularly small. In Australia there are more than 20,000 species of moth, with wingspans ranging from 3 mm to more than 250 mm. The great majority of moths are tiny, called microlepidoptera, and are small enough to feed within a single leaf or flower without running out of food and without being disturbed by predators.

Right: Most moths are very small. Called microlepidoptera, they make up the great majority of moth species.

the FACTS!

THE LARGEST insects in the world weigh twenty times more than the world's smallest mammal, the Etruscan Shrew.

MUCH SIZE VARIATION exists among insects. The biggest beetle in the world is more than 18 million times bigger than the smallest beetle.

THE BEETLE family Ptilidae contains hundreds of species, all smaller than a millimetre in length.

THE LARGEST LIVING INSECT species, or those that weigh the most, are the giant scarab and longicorn beetles from Africa and South America.

BASED ON OVERALL LENGTH, the smallest adult insect in the world is a parasitic wasp, *Dicopomorpha echmepterygis*. Males of this species are blind and wingless and measure only 0.14 mm in length.

VERY SMALL INSECTS find it as difficult to move through air as we do to move through water. Consequently, very small flying insects may have oar-shaped wings.

THE LARGEST INSECTS that ever lived were probably dragonflies of the Permian or Triassic Periods (about 250 million years ago), which had a wingspan up to 750 mm.

Biology of spiders

What makes a spider?

Above: Although most spiders have small eyes that do not see well, some species, such as net-casting spiders, have large eyes with excellent vision.

Centre, right: Spiders' eyes are grouped in characteristic patterns at the front and sides of the cephalothorax.

Spiders are a truly magnificent group of creatures and are major contributors to Australian ecosystems, but they have long been treated with fear and disgust by the public and with neglect by scientists.

ALMOST EVERYWHERE insects have established in Australia, spiders have also carved themselves a niche. Their habitats range from deserts to caves, streams to seashores and alpine country to rainforests. Most of the species that live here are restricted to Australia, but some are also found overseas and several species have been introduced from Australia to other countries.

30,000 SPECIES of spiders have been described throughout the world; more than 2000 of those are found in Australia. It is estimated this is only one quarter of the number that actually exist. Australian spiders range in size from the 55 mm-long bird-eating spiders, to litter-dwelling spiders that measure less than a millimetre.

the FACTS!

SPIDERS ARE KNOWN as arachnids, named after the maiden Arachne from Greek Mythology. According to legend she was a skilled weaver who was changed into a spider as punishment for pride in her own cleverness.

MANY SPIDERS show maternal care for their young. A female wolf spider carries around her egg sac behind her abdomen until the eggs hatch, when the spiderlings climb onto her back (below).

THE EGGS of spiders contain more yolk than the eggs of most insects. This enables spiderlings to develop further within the egg and emerge at a more advanced stage of growth.

SPIDERS CAN WALK UP GLASS and across ceilings because of thick tufts of hairs at the ends of their legs. Each tuft may contain 1000 tiny individual hairs. The structure of these tufts also helps some spiders walk across water.

WHAT MAKES A SPIDER?

Spiders differ from insects by having two body parts instead of three, joined by a narrow waist. The first part is a fusion of the head and middle section (together called the "cephalothorax"), which bears the eyes, mouthparts and legs and is covered with a shield-like carapace. The second part is the abdomen, containing reproductive and digestive organs, silk glands and the spinnerets that produce and shape the silk. At the front of the head are the fangs: hollow, needle-like structures used to capture and kill prey, and for defence. With few exceptions, all spiders are venomous to their prey, but only three of four species are venomous to humans.

Behind the fangs are a pair of appendages (pedipalps) that basically act as touch receptors. Mature males bear enlarged sex organs at the end of the pedipalps, which are waved at the female during courtship displays. These organs are the major external difference between males and females, but females are also generally larger than males. The next four pairs of appendages are walking legs, variable in form and function, but generally simple and unspecialised.

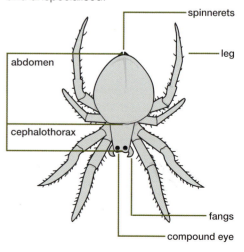

Above: A spider's body has two distinct parts — the cephalothorax that supports the legs; and the smooth cylindrical abdomen.

Above: A *Dolophones* spider camouflaged on a tree trunk. The spider will hold this position, even when directly threatened.

CONSERVATION WATCH

Twenty-three species of spider are of conservation concern in Australia. Four are protected by law in Tasmania (including two species thought to be extinct), as well as ten species in Western Australia, mostly trapdoor spiders.

Spiders play an immensely important role in the ecology of most Australian environments because of the food they provide to a wide range of predators and because they help to control insect populations. These controls are especially important in farming areas where, without spiders, insect pests would cause far greater crop losses than they currently do.

Above: Newly hatched huntsmen clustering on their egg sac. At this time of life they are at their most vulnerable.

FISHING FOR PREY

All spiders are carnivores and they will also become cannibals if the opportunity arises. Spiders will prey on anything of appropriate size, including most invertebrates and some small fish, reptiles, birds and even mammals. In comparison to their own size, spiders have the largest range of prey sizes in the animal kingdom. The Golden Orb-weaver (*Nephila ornata*) feeds on almost anything trapped in its net, from the tiniest midges to small birds.

Almost all spiders live solitary, transient lives, sensitive to changes in the environment and to predator and prey densities. In some animal communities they are the dominant predator in the food chain. Studies of spider numbers show that up to 842 spiders per square metre may be present in foliage. This number may be even higher around pasture and crops.

Spiders demonstrate some amazing adaptations for capturing prey. The Bird-dropping Spider (*Celaenia kinbergi*) mimics female moth pheromones to attract male moths to their deaths. Net-casting Spiders (*Deinopis subrufa*) weave tiny nets that they cast over insects that come within their reach. Fishing spiders (*Dolomedes* spp.) dive under water in search of aquatic prey, while the Bolas Spider (*Ordgarius monstrosus*) swings a sticky blob at the end of a silk thread to capture passing insects. Some spiders (such as *Myrmarachne* spp.) are accomplished mimics of ants, which allows them to move undetected among their prey. Some spiders sit and wait for prey (called the ambushers or web-spinners), while others actively hunt and run down their prey (the hunters).

Right: Ground-dwelling wolf spiders may be so perfectly patterned that they are indistinguishable from their surroundings.

the FACTS!

SPIDERS DISPERSE by ballooning away on a thread of silk. Some spiders have been collected by planes flying at high altitudes over the middle of the ocean.

SOME SPIDERS erect and defend mobile or stationary territories, while others disperse from an area if it becomes overpopulated.

MALE SPIDERS are short-lived, usually living a year or so, but females of some species may live more than twenty years. Consequently, spider populations may be dominated by mature females.

SPIDERS CAN have an impact on insect populations without directly consuming them. When spiders are present, plant-eating insects may abandon their food plants and starve to death as a result.

Catching food
— dinner time

Above: Using its web, the Red-back Spider is able to capture prey several times its own size.

LIVING IN AUSTRALIA

The warmer climate over much of Australia enables spiders to grow larger and faster than in many of the cooler parts of the world. The Garden Wolf Spider (*Geolycosa godeffroyi*) grows to 40 times the weight of similar wolf spiders in Europe (such as *Pardosa lugubris*) over the same period of time. The heat may cause other problems, however, and Australian spiders must also avoid high day temperatures, fierce bushfires and drought conditions.

RARELY DO SPIDERS live in an area of constant food supply. To overcome food shortages, spiders have a range of ingenious adaptations. They have abdomens that are able to stretch enormously to accommodate a sudden increase in food; they are also able to store large amounts of fat. Wolf spiders generally consume only 2–3% of their body weight each day, but will readily consume up to 10% of their weight if the opportunity arises. Spiders have a very low metabolism and are able to continue to operate as predators on only one fifth of their normal energy requirements.

When food is scarce, a spider will move its web or increase its territory to boost the chances of encountering prey. Web-building species may change the orientation of the web, or move it higher in foliage or to a different location altogether. Burrowing spiders will abandon their holes and take up territory in a more fruitful position. Young spiders may take longer to reach adulthood or even mature at a smaller size without sufficient food, but will reach maturity nonetheless. Consequently, the number of eggs produced will be much lower, but there will always be enough offspring to keep the population going.

Centre, top to bottom: Crab spiders demonstrate remarkable camouflage. This one is hiding on bark; Ambushers such as crab spiders hide among flowers to trap visiting pollinators such as skipper butterflies. *Below:* This moulting huntsman will require a couple of hours for its new skin to dry before it can move around normally.

EAT OR BE EATEN

There are many types of tiny flies and wasps that are parasites on spiders. These parasites may attack the eggs, spiderlings or adult spiders and, although the parasites do not kill their host immediately, they will almost always kill it in the end. Spiders are also eaten by some insects, scorpions, centipedes, fish, frogs, reptiles, birds and mammals.

the FACTS!

WITH CAREFUL management, spiders have been used to control pest insect populations in glasshouses and other situations.

SPIDERS ARE OFTEN the most numerous predators in any land-based ecosystem. Unlike many predatory insects, spiders usually have a permanent presence in most habitats.

SPIDERS are known as generalist predators and will try to capture and consume any prey of suitable size. This adaptation is probably a result of surviving for millions of years with a general shortage of prey.

MANY SPIDERS PRODUCE both fertile and infertile eggs in any clutch. The infertile eggs are eaten by the spiderlings soon after they hatch.

GOLDEN ORB-WEAVERS (*Nephila ornata*) may produce more than 3000 eggs in a single egg sac. Only a very small proportion of these survive to maturity.

SPIDERS FREQUENTLY eat other spiders and even members of their own species. They will feed on eggs, spiderlings and potential mating partners, and some species even consume their own mothers.

Spider webs
— silken artistry

Silk is used by many types of invertebrates, from ants to caterpillars, but spiders have made silk production into an art form. Spider silk is best known for its use in prey capture, not only in web-building but also in the construction of trip lines (burrowing spiders), as a net (net-casting spiders), as a safety line while hunting (huntsmen) and as a smothering device to wrap dangerous prey.

SILK IS ALSO used to line burrows, build shelters and protect spiders during the delicate process of moulting. Female spiders may use silk to build a safe shelter while producing eggs or may even wrap their eggs in silken egg sacs for further protection. Silk is used by males to transfer sperm to the female during mating. It is also used by the males of some species to tie the female down during courtship.

Above: The classical circular structure of an orb-weaver's web.

Left: Like many spiders, female clubionid spiders use silk to build both egg sacs and shelters in which to lay her eggs.

DIFFERENT SILK FOR DIFFERENT JOBS

Each type of spider may produce a different type of silk that is designed in its texture, thickness and stickiness to be perfectly suited to a particular job. For example, a single web may be composed of very strong, dry silk that makes up the basic frame, finer threads that radiate out from the centre, and special sticky silk that makes up the spiral which traps prey.

Spiders are not trapped in their own webs, but may become trapped in the webs of other spiders. The bodies of most spiders are coated with an oil that prevents them becoming stuck, but if the oil is rubbed off, the spider may become entangled. As an added precaution, much of the framework of a spider's web is made of non-sticky silk so the spider can move freely around the web and avoid the sticky threads.

A TRULY REMARKABLE FIBRE

Spider silk is one of the strongest known natural fibres — five times stronger than steel and much more flexible. Depending on the type of silk, it can be stretched to more than twice its own length and is excellent at absorbing energy, enabling the spider to sit safely in the centre of its web. Humans have been trying for many years to replicate spider silk in the laboratory, so far without success.

Some spiders build an extra structure at the centre of the web, called a "stabilimentum". This may be circular, X-shaped, or a single line horizontally or vertically through the hub.

Below: Some webs can be extremely elaborate, with several silken platforms at different heights.

the FACTS!

SPIDER SILK apparently evolved very early in spiders' development. It is first thought to have been used to line spiders' burrows and protect eggs from drying out.

SILK IS MADE up of 50% protein, which is a key to its strength. No other natural or artificial material with such a high protein component can be spun into a thin thread like spider silk can.

SPIDER SILK can stop a honeybee travelling at 25 km/h without breaking. A giant web with silk the width of a pencil could effortlessly stop a jumbo jet at full speed.

UNLIKE ARTIFICIAL FIBRES, silk does not lose its properties when frozen. It will not break even when kept at temperatures of −40°C.

SPIDERLINGS use long strands of silk to catch the breeze and lift them into the air. This behaviour, called "ballooning", can transport them more than 4 km into the atmosphere and disperse the spiderlings many thousands of kilometres.

TRAPDOOR SPIDERS incorporate soil and leaf litter into a silken lid for their burrow. The combination of materials makes the trapdoor very solid and it may last many years.

Above: Many spiders construct a silken moulting chamber in which to shed their skin.

MAKING SILK

Silk is produced by "spinnerets" at the tip of the abdomen. There are usually three pairs of spinnerets and their size and arrangement varies among the different spider families. In most spiders, the spinnerets can be seen just protruding from the tip of the abdomen, but some groups, such as tailed spiders, may have exceptionally long spinnerets. Each spinneret is attached to a silk gland and there are seven known types of silk glands, each producing a different type of silk. Some spiders have a special plate (cribellum) between the spinnerets which causes the silk to be drawn out in broad bands of tangled threads.

Silk is produced as a liquid within the silk gland, squeezed out like toothpaste from a tube. The spider draws silk out with its back legs and the strength of the silk may be determined by how hard the spider pulls on it. The silk we see is actually a combination of a number of strands, together as little as 0.0003 mm thick. Spiders such as the Garden Orb-weaver (*Eriophora transmarina*) consume the web at the end of the night, recycling the precious protein locked up in the silk, as well as picking up the tiny flies and pollen grains stuck in the silk that it otherwise would have missed.

the FACTS!

ALL SPIDERS have at least three different types of silk glands. Garden Orb-weavers (*Eriophora transmarina*) and Golden Orb-weavers (*Nephila* sp.) each have five different types. No species possesses all seven possible types of silk.

SILK IS OFTEN CLEAR but it can come in a range of colours, including green, blue, brown and black. Some spiders produce silver or golden silk, which catches the sunlight to provide a magnificent display.

THE FLOW of silk from the spinnerets is controlled by tiny valves called "spigots". Up to 600 spigots are under the control of a single spider when it releases silk.

Above: Spiders commonly decorate their webs with the bodies of old prey. The spider is well disguised in the centre.

HIGH FLYING SPIDERS

In 2003, a group of Australian high school students sent Garden Orb-weavers (*Eriophora transmarina*) into space on the Space Shuttle Colombia to determine whether the spiders could build webs in zero gravity. They found that the spiders were not deterred by the lack of gravity and built perfect orb webs to capture tiny fruit flies. The size and structure of the webs appeared to be identical to those built by other members of the same species on the ground.

The silk itself was of particular interest to scientists, who have for many years been trying to make artificial spider silk. Given that there is no artificial material that comes close to the strength and flexibility of the fibre spun by spiders, any breakthrough in this area could revolutionise the materials we use. Fibres constructed in space often naturally form differently to those constructed on Earth, giving insights into how to make them artificially. Unfortunately for the spiders and the astronauts, the shuttle Colombia broke up on re-entry to Earth and the silk built in space was also destroyed. The search for the perfect artificial fibre continues.

Right: This is a photograph taken on a different space mission from that described above. It shows an American spider's initial attempt at weaving her web in a weightless environment before she adapted to zero gravity.

Mygalomorphs
— primitive spiders

Class: Arachnida
Order: Aranae **Infraorder:** Mygalomorphae

Spiders are classified in the order Aranae, which is divided into two groups: the "primitive" spiders (mygalomorphs) and the "advanced" spiders (araneomorphs).

THE MAJOR DISTINCTION between the two groups is the way their fangs move. The fangs of primitive spiders strike downward like daggers, whereas those of advanced spiders move sidewards against each other like pincers. Primitive spiders therefore often rear up before striking. They cannot live in webs suspended among leaves because they need a solid surface to grip when striking.

TALL, DARK & HAIRY

The primitive spiders include funnelwebs, trapdoor spiders and bird-eating spiders. They are all generally large, dark and hairy, long-lived and ground-dwelling. Most types spend almost all their time in burrows or under logs, but a couple of species live in holes in tree trunks. Different types of primitive spiders tend to look very similar to each other and have similar lifestyles.

THERE MAY BE UP TO 40 DIFFERENT types of funnelwebs in Australia, but the Sydney Funnelweb (*Atrax robustus*) is found only around the Sydney region. Funnelwebs generally need to live in cool moist areas with plenty of rainfall.

NOT ALL TRAPDOOR SPIDERS build trapdoors on their burrows; many live under logs or in open burrows. Trapdoor spiders are more adaptable to different environments than other primitive spiders; they can be common in most habitats in Australia and may even be abundant in suburban areas.

THERE ARE A NUMBER of different types of bird-eating spiders (mostly living in northern Australia) and they belong to the same family as the tarantulas from overseas. These are the largest spiders in Australia.

Above: Mouse spiders may be found across Australia. This female has formidable fangs.

Left: Funnelweb spider.

ADAPTABLE & WIDESPREAD

The advanced spiders are by far the largest and most conspicuous group of spiders, being colourful and often bizarre in shape, and displaying a wide array of lifestyles and habits. Because they do not need to strike downwards on their prey like primitive spiders, they can hunt for prey on unstable surfaces such as leaves and even flimsy webs suspended high among trees. This has enabled them to colonise most habitats and niches on Earth.

Left: A trapdoor spider emerging from its burrow. Many trapdoor species do not actually construct a trapdoor on their burrows.

the FACTS!

APART FROM their common names, there is little that separates trapdoor spiders from funnelwebs. Almost nothing is known of their life histories and many species have not even been named or described.

THE BIGGEST spiders in the world are mygalomorphs and all belong to the tarantula family. The Goliath Tarantula from South America may grow to 270 mm across the legs.

MYGALOMORPHS TAKE a long time to reach maturity and the females live for many years. Although males are short-lived, the record for a female is more than 23 years.

THE MOST VENOMOUS spider in the world is the Sydney Funnelweb (*Atrax robustus*). Until an antivenom was produced, thirteen people had died following bites.

IN NORTH Queensland, male bird-eating spiders (*Selenocosmia* sp.) wander into houses at the start of summer as they look for females.

A GROUP of primitive spiders called hypochilomorphs appear to be a living link between mygalomorphs and araneomorphs. The Tasmanian Cave Spider (*Hickmania troglodytes*) is a member of this group.

Hunters
— huntsmen, wolf spiders & others

Above: Huntsmen will eat any insect prey small enough to be overpowered. A caterpillar is easy prey for this specimen. *Below:* Wolf spiders are active, free-ranging spiders that generally return to a burrow or other form of permanent retreat.

Class: Arachnida
Order: Aranae

Hunting spiders include huntsmen, wolf spiders, lynx spiders and sac spiders. Hunting spiders may have a territory that they continuously patrol or else they may be nomadic, ranging over wide areas in search of prey. Many do not build a permanent retreat but spin shelters only when necessary (to moult or lay eggs). Others spin a permanent silken tube from which they base their hunting activities. Most are nocturnal and can be fast-moving when necessary. Hunting spiders can be found patrolling foliage or tree trunks, wandering across the ground or even living inside our houses.

VERSATILE WOLVES

Wolf spiders are the dominant family of ground-dwelling spiders in Australia. They are characterised by a row of small eyes at the front of the head and four much larger eyes above, which give them excellent vision. With their long legs they run down their prey on the ground. Many species are burrowers and their holes are common in suburban backyards around Australia. Wolf spider burrows can be found almost anywhere — from along the high-tide line of beaches to swamps, sandy and pebble deserts, and above the snow line in the mountains. Few groups of spiders can survive in such a wide range of habitats.

the FACTS!

LIKE OWLS and possums, wolf spiders have a mirror-like structure at the back of the eye that reflects light. At night under torchlight, wolf spiders' eyes seem to light up.

WOLF SPIDERS often have distinctive patterns on their backs. The common Garden Wolf Spider (*Geolycosa godeffroyi*) has a radiating pattern on its cephalothorax similar to the Union Jack on the British flag.

THE FORREST Wolf Spider (*Lycosa forresti*) is one of the few species of wolf spider that builds doors on its burrow. In this species, the colour of the spider can vary depending on the colour of the soil where it lives.

HUNTSMEN are readily spread around the country by humans, particularly in cars. Cars make a good home for huntsmen and their sudden appearance is said to be the cause of some traffic accidents.

SLOW-MOVING HUNTERS

Huntsmen are a very well-known group of spiders — due to their habit of living inside houses. Most species naturally live under bark or logs, or in rock crevices. Because of their flattened bodies and the fact that the legs are twisted sideways to the body and point towards the front, huntsmen are able to squeeze through tiny cracks and live happily in very confined spaces. They spend most of their time motionless and, even when on the move, tend to move very slowly. They feed on any insect of suitable size, particularly cockroaches and crickets.

A GAGGLE OF HUNTERS

Many hunters belong to small and less well-known families of spiders. The family Corinnidae includes the spider *Supunna albopunctata*, which does not produce any web. These spiders are black and white with orange legs and move very rapidly over the ground, particularly in hot weather, feeding on ground-dwelling prey.

The spiders of genus *Rebilus*, in the family Gnaphosidae, live under bark or loose slabs of stone. They feed on a wide variety of insects and other spiders but, like most Australian hunting spiders, little is known about them. Within the same family, *Hemicloea* sp. is a larger spider that looks similar to huntsmen but is shiny black or brown. The family Zodariidae includes a very attractive spider (*Storena formosa*) that lives in Australia's dry inland. It has beautiful red legs and a black and white patterned body.

Left: Badge spiders are a type of huntsman that search for prey among foliage. They have a shield-shaped badge underneath the abdomen.

Above, left to right: Nursery web spiders hunt insects on the water surface and are able to run across ponds with remarkable speed; *Rebilus* sp. has a much flattened body that enables it to live under bark and flat rocks; Zodariids are wandering spiders — this species (*Storena* sp.), often wanders into rural houses at night in search of prey.

SAC DWELLING SPIDERS

Sac spiders (such as *Cheiracanthium* spp., left) have a large pair of jaws and get their common name from their habit of building silken envelopes between sewn-together leaves. The retreat becomes a brood chamber during summer when the female lays eggs. She dies soon afterwards. The closely related *Clubiona robusta* builds similar retreats under bark. Both are vagrant hunters that feed on wandering insects. Sac spiders are known to give a painful bite. The Miturga (*Miturga* sp.) is a large spider that is similar in appearance to the wolf spiders; it builds large silken retreats (up to 100 mm long) in grass tussocks.

the FACTS!

IN RURAL AREAS, huntsmen are often misnamed "tarantulas". They are also given the characteristically Australian name "triantelopes". Their most unusual name is "triontywantigons".

FEMALE HUNTSMEN are unusual among spiders in that they are not aggressive towards the males. Mating may take up to seven hours, during which the spiders spend much of the time stroking each others' legs.

FEMALE huntsmen usually guard the egg sac and open the tough silk to let the spiderlings out once they have hatched. Many species guard the young after they have hatched and even share prey with them.

THE AGGRESSIVE, fast-moving hunter *Supunna* is itself attacked by a small species of parasitic wasp. The wasp lays its eggs into the spider's body and the wasp larvae feed on the spider from the inside.

BADGE SPIDERS are a type of orange or green huntsman that can give a painful bite. They are named after the shield-shaped markings underneath their abdomens.

STORENA HUNTING SPIDERS, which live in open, stony areas, build turrets of pebbles around the nest. This is thought to be a way to stop the nest from flooding.

WHITE-TAILED VILLAINS

The White-tailed Spider (*Lampona cylindrata*) occurs all over Australia and New Zealand. In the wild they live under bark or stones, but also favour the cool, dry conditions inside houses. White-tailed Spiders are vagrant hunters and may be commonly seen roaming walls at night in search of insects and other spiders. They seem to feed particularly on Black House Spiders (*Badumna insignis*), also common in houses. White-tailed Spiders have an undeserved reputation for causing serious illness and even deaths in humans, but there is no evidence that the bite of this species causes any symptoms other than headaches and local itching.

Above: Miturgid spider.

Below: White-tailed Spider.

Ambushers
— crab spiders, red-backs & others

Class: Arachnida
Order: Aranae

Right: A flower spider perched on a flower. The two pairs of back legs anchor the spider to the flower; the other pairs are held apart awaiting flying insects.

Bottom: Crab spiders typically sit with the first two pairs of spined legs held wide open, ready to close on prey that approaches too closely.

the FACTS!

WHEN MOVING across a tree trunk, Two-tailed Spiders hold their long spinnerets off the bark to prevent them being damaged.

CRAB SPIDERS have excellent vision and are unusual among spiders in being able to move each eye independently of the others.

BECAUSE OF THE funnel-shaped retreat in the back of a Black House Spider's (*Badumna insignis*) web, these spiders are sometimes confused with funnelweb spiders. They are, however, unrelated.

CRAB SPIDERS (below) are named for their crab-like shape and their habit of scuttling sideways. When moving, they anchor themselves with a silken drag line.

A GROUP OF crab spiders that live on tree trunks (*Stephanopis* spp.) are superbly camouflaged. They enhance this camouflage by attaching tiny flakes of bark to their backs.

Several families of spiders may be considered ambushers. These spiders tend to sit and wait for prey rather than actively chasing it.

ONE OF THE LARGEST FAMILIES is the crab spiders. Spiders in one group of the family, called flower spiders, are sometimes coloured yellow or red to match the flowers upon which they hunt, although many are pure white. A flower spider will sit on a flower anchored by its back two pairs of legs, with the front two pairs opened to grasp flying insects that land on the flower. If a fly, bee or even butterfly lands, the spider grabs the insect and bites it on the back of the neck, sucking out its body fluids. Most species are territorial, spending all their time on one or two flowers, moving only when the flower dies.

CASTING THE NET

Few animals demonstrate such a remarkable prey-capturing technique as the net-casting spiders. They have a long narrow body and greatly enlarged eyes for detecting prey (right). Balanced on long, stick-like legs, they sit above insect pathways at night and hold out a rectangular silken net that is thrown over any prey, including moths on the wing, which comes within reach. The net is made from a highly expandable silk that can be stretched to ten times its normal size. Once prey is caught, the spider consumes it through the net and constructs a new net. If an unused net is left over at the end of the night, the spider hangs it between twigs to be used again the following evening.

Ambushers

Far left, top to bottom: This crab spider, *Runcinia* sp., is a common sight on grass heads across eastern Australia; Most crab spiders are quite small — the Spectacular Crab Spider is one of the largest, big enough to entrap honeybees and large butterflies; The web of the Red-back Spider includes very strong strands attached to the ground — prey that contact the strands are catapulted into the web.

RED-BACKED ICON

One of the best known spiders in Australia is the Red-back Spider (*Latrodectus hasselti*, above). Like other spiders that build snares, Red-back Spiders construct a messy web in corners with a retreat for the spider in the rear. These webs are often known as cobwebs. Sticky silken traplines radiate out from the web and are attached to nearby features; when an insect blunders into a trapline it becomes stuck fast. These traplines are exceptionally strong, powerful enough to hold small skinks or mice. The web is usually built close to the ground and this species is commonly found in garden sheds and abandoned buildings. When alerted to trapped prey, the spider runs down the web and subdues the prey by wrapping it thickly in its web before injecting its powerful venom.

A WORLD OF SNARES

Many other types of spiders build snares or ambush their prey in other ways. Bird-dropping Spiders (*Celaenia kinbergi*) sit in foliage at night and attract male moths with a pheromone that is almost identical to the pheromone released by female moths to attract partners for mating. Black House Spiders (*Badumna insignis*) are common in all Australian States and live inside houses, feeding on flies and moths. They are also known as

Above: Black House Spider.
Below left: A typical Black House Spider's web.

Window Spiders for their habit of building messy webs in the corners of windows. The dense white silk of the web is shaped into a funnel leading to a retreat for the spider at the back of the web. The front of the web opens out to curtain-like sheets of silk that may extend for 350 mm from the retreat; these are used for trapping prey.

the FACTS!

MALE NET-CASTING SPIDERS use nets to capture prey as they grow, but abandon their nets when mature to search for a female. The male dies soon after mating.

THE NET of a net-casting spider is about the size of a small postage stamp. The frame of the web is made from dry silk and the rest comprises zigzagging rows of sticky silk from the cribellum.

FEMALE RED-BACK SPIDERS are one of the most deadly spiders in the world, having caused at least thirteen deaths in Australia. The fangs of the male are too small to penetrate human skin.

RED-BACK SPIDERS have readily adapted to living with humans. They were common in the old outback dunnies and a large proportion of bites were inflicted upon unsuspecting visitors to the toilet.

SPIDERS ARE one of Australia's many exports. Some types of house spiders (*Badumna* spp.) have been accidentally introduced to New Zealand and California and Red-back Spiders (*Latrodectus hasselti*) have made their way to Japan.

Orb-weavers
— champion spinners

Class: Arachnida
Order: Aranae

The master web spinners in the spider world are undoubtedly the orb-weavers. With minimal silk and maximal skill, they build perfectly symmetrical circular webs that may span many metres and trap hundreds of flying insects. The web may be removed by the spider and rebuilt each day, or may be moved to a new location if the flying insect traffic is insufficient.

Above: Orb-weavers are able to use their enormous webs to trap large prey that they would otherwise be unable to overpower.

Right: The Golden Orb-weaver is a familiar sight over much of eastern Australia.

the FACTS!

ORB WEAVING spiders may produce more than 20 m of silk to construct a single web. These webs can be strong enough to support more than 4000 times the collective weight of the spider and its prey.

THE POWDERY SCALES on moth wings are thought to be an adaptation against spider webs. If trapped in a web, the moth may shed some scales and fly safely away.

UNLIKE HUNTING SPIDERS, orb-weavers are unable to drink free water. Many species get their water requirements by consuming the web just before dawn, picking up water from dew.

NATURE'S ARCHITECTS

Orb webs are complicated structures that are built with remarkable simplicity. They begin with a single strand of silk that is released by the spider and drawn out by a breeze until it attaches to a solid object. The spider pulls the thread tight and uses it as the basis for the rest of the web. A non-sticky framework is then constructed below this thread in the shape of the letter "Y", usually with the base of the web touching the ground.

The spider then fills in the rest of the web with spokes that radiate out from the centre, or hub, of the web. Once this stage is complete, the spider adds a continuous line of sticky spirals that move from the edge of the web to the hub. As the spider moves, it collects some of the dry web that previously was used as scaffolding during the orb's construction and consumes it. The spider avoids being trapped in its own silk by moving only along the non-sticky parts of the web.

VARIATIONS ON A SUCCESSFUL THEME

The least complicated form of orb web is the perfectly symmetrical variety. However, many orb-weavers have developed variations on this theme and some groups have lost the ability to build orb webs altogether, having developed even more successful and specialised means of capturing prey.

Leaf-Curling Spiders (*Phonognatha graeffei*, right) have added a shelter at the top of the web, usually made from a leaf or similar object, in which they are less vulnerable to predators. A number of species, including the Tailed Spider (*Arachnura* sp.), decorate their webs with long lines of objects such as discarded prey. Many species add lines of zigzagging silk in various patterns (called a "stabilimentum"). Jewel Spiders (*Austracantha minax*) lace their orb webs together in congregations that may cover large areas. This species also attaches white tufts of silk to the web, but the reason for this is unknown.

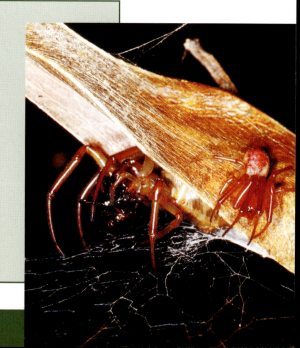

CONSERVATION WATCH

Six species of harvestmen are of conservation concern in Australia. All of these are cave-dwelling species from Tasmania and five are from a single genus: *Hickmanoxyomma*.

Above: Triangular spiders behave more like crab spiders than orb-weavers. The structure of the body, however, is the same as other orb weaving spiders.

Left: The web of this St Andrew's Cross Spider from southern Australia is characterised by an x-shaped pattern of silk, called a stabilimentum, that passes through the hub.

SITTING ON THE FENCE

Once an orb web is built, the spider must decide which side to sit on. In areas of high wind, the spider may prefer to sit with its back to the wind to avoid being blown off. Others will make their choice based on the available light, temperature or the abundance of prey. The St Andrew's Cross Spider (*Argiope keyserlingi*) builds webs close to bushes and sits with its back to the light, presumably to prevent predators such as mantids sneaking up on it from within the foliage.

THE ORIGINAL RECYCLERS

Some spiders, particularly orb-weavers such as the Garden Orb-weaver (*Eriophora transmarina*), will spin webs at night then eat the entire web before dawn the next day. There are several reasons for this. Firstly, silk is full of protein and a large web represents a massive energy investment for a spider. During the day the web is likely to be destroyed by birds or other animals stumbling into it. Secondly, when insects are caught in webs they often cause considerable damage before being subdued and it is often easier to replace the entire web rather than repair all the damage. Thirdly, the spider picks up a considerable quantity of food and water by eating the web. Spiders receive up to one tenth of their water intake from moisture absorbed by the sticky glue on the web and they also consume all the tiny insects that are stuck in the web and which are too small to pick off individually.

Above: St Andrew's Cross Spiders sit in the centre of the web with legs held in pairs — in the shape of a cross.

the FACTS!

THE FIRST SPECIES of spider described from Australia was an orb-weaver, the Spiny Spider (*Gasteracantha fornicata*) from north Queensland. It was described by Fabricius in 1775.

GOLDEN ORB-WEAVERS (*Nephila* sp.) may build vast curtains of webs between power lines during summer. The masses of golden silk pick up the afternoon light and are a spectacular sight.

SOME WEBS ARE STRONG enough to trap small birds. Wrens and silvereyes are sometimes caught in the webs of Golden Orb-weavers and the spiders will readily feed on them.

ORB WEBS MAY be visible to some flying insects that can see them from up to 100 mm away and steer clear. Many spiders build their webs in areas of poor light to make their silk traps harder to see.

THE HUB of a web is usually built closer to the top of the web than the bottom. This is because, once prey has become trapped, it takes the spider longer to run uphill than downhill.

WHEN BUILDING A WEB, the spider uses its hindleg to pull each thread taut once complete. This breaks up the sticky coating into minute globules like beads on a necklace.

Above: The large, bulbous eyes of this jumping spider give it excellent 360° vision.

Below: Some jumping spiders have long, thin bodies. Others, like this one, are quite stocky.

Jumping spiders
— great leaps, keen eyes

Class: Arachnida
Order: Aranae

Jumping spiders are perhaps the most common spiders in Australia, found in just about every habitat. They are highly active, moving constantly in short dashes or longer leaps. Even when at rest, the cephalothorax is continuously moving as the spider keeps an eye out for predators or passing prey.

THE EYES HAVE IT

Like many other spiders, jumping spiders have eight eyes in two rows at the front of the cephalothorax. The middle pair at the front, however, can be enormous, giving jumping spiders excellent vision. When the smaller eyes detect movement, the larger eyes are turned to focus on potential prey. Because of the positioning of the eyes on the cephalothorax, jumping spiders have 360° vision. They can also move swiftly in any direction.

the FACTS!

JUMPING SPIDERS form the largest family of spiders in the world. There are more than 250 known species in Australia and more than 5000 species worldwide.

MOST JUMPING SPIDERS are about 4–8 mm long. The largest in Australia is the Green Jumping Spider (*Mopsus mormon*), which measures 12 mm long.

JUMPING SPIDERS include the most colourful spiders in the world. Australian species are adorned with greens, reds, blues, silver and gold.

THE MALES of some Australian jumping spiders (such as *Helpis minitabunda*) have large fangs that they use to fight off other males for the right to mate with females.

THE MALE FLYING SPIDER (*Maratus volans*), found in New South Wales, has flaps on the sides of the abdomen that were once thought to assist in gliding. These flaps are now known to be used during courtship.

DANCING SPIDERS

The magnificent range of colours displayed by jumping spiders is used to full extent during courtship. The male will raise his colourful abdomen like a peacock's tail and stand on the tips of his legs, gliding across a leaf in front of a female. Jumping spider courtship dances are the most complicated and spectacular in the arachnid world, if not the animal kingdom. The dance may be accompanied by sound, generated by vibrating the leaf surface as it moves or by rubbing hairs from the abdomen over the back of the cephalothorax. Courtship may continue for long periods before the female allows the male to come close enough to mate.

Above: The male Green Jumping Spider, the largest jumping spider in Australia, has a line of white hairs down each side of the cephalothorax. *Below, left:* Many jumping spiders are brilliantly coloured and are sometimes referred to as "peacock spiders".

SPIDERY ANTS

Ant-mimicking jumping spiders (*Myrmarachne* spp.) hang around ant trails and pick off wayward ants. Like all spiders, these species have only two body parts, but the abdomen has a constriction in the middle so the spider looks like it has three body parts (like all insects). The front pair of legs are held out in front of the spider, not only appearing as antennae but apparently giving the spiders three pairs of legs instead of four.

Other arachnids
— scorpions, mites & others

STING IN THE TAIL

Scorpions are well known for having a long segmented tail that ends in a sting. They can be extremely venomous in some parts of the world, but Australian species are relatively harmless. Australian scorpions also tend to be smaller than those overseas, although some species may grow up to 120 mm long. Females give birth to live young, which immediately climb onto their mother's back and are carried around for several weeks before leaving to continue their lives independently.

Above: Desert scorpions are a common feature of Australia's arid areas. They spend most of their time underground in very deep, spiralling burrows.

PSEUDOSCORPIONS

A group of arachnids that resemble scorpions but lack the tail are called pseudoscorpions (false scorpions). Pseudoscorpions are typically small; usually much less than 10 mm long. They have a venom gland in the pincers that is used to kill prey such as small insects and spiders living under bark. Pseudoscorpions have a habit of hitch-hiking on animals larger than themselves, usually insects, in order to get around.

THE MIGHTY MITES

Mites are a very diverse group, living in freshwater and marine environments, and on land. Many are predatory, feeding on other mites or insects, while others feed on plants and can be serious pests of crops. Some mites are parasitic, feeding on the fluids of insects or inside the nasal passages and lungs of vertebrates, including mammals. In many habitats, mites are as common and as important to the ecosystem as insects.

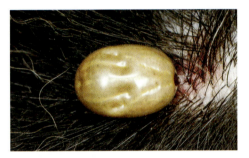

Above: Australian ticks attach themselves to a range of native mammals, as well as domestic animals such as dogs.

A BIG TICK FROM MITES

Ticks are closely related to mites and are physically almost identical. They differ, however, because, as a group, they are all designed to feed on the blood of vertebrates, including humans. Ticks tend to be larger than mites, although the size of each tick varies dramatically depending on how much it has fed. The eggs are normally laid in soil and the newly hatched nymphs are left to find their own hosts. The great majority of these never do.

PSEUDO-SPIDERS

Harvestmen are sometimes called Daddy Longlegs but they are very different to spiders of that name. Harvestmen are round-bodied, while spiders have two body parts separated by a thin waist. Most species of harvestmen live in leaf litter or under logs. They are most common in the wetter areas of Australia.

Left: Most mites are too small to be seen with the naked eye, but a few species are conspicuously large.

the FACTS!

BABY SCORPIONS are generally able to protect themselves with their stings, but they spend their first couple of weeks of life riding on their mother's back. If one baby falls off, the mother will stop and wait for it to climb back aboard.

OF THE 1200 or so scorpions known throughout the world, only about 50 species are dangerous to humans. No Australian scorpions are known to cause a fatal sting.

HARVESTMEN (below) usually feed on small insects and spiders but are unable to produce silk. Some species feed on plant material or the bodies of dead birds.

UNLIKE SCORPIONS, spiders and their other relatives, male harvestmen have a long penis and mate directly with females. The females are also unusual in that they possess ovipositors and lay eggs directly into the soil.

Crustaceans
— insects of the sea

the FACTS!

THE MANTIS SHRIMP has an extension to its claw that can be flicked out to knock out prey. This is one of the fastest actions in the animal kingdom, with the same velocity as a .22 calibre bullet.

SMALL CRAB SPECIES living on coral reefs sometimes attach sea anemones to their backs, or carry them around in their claws. The anemones have stinging tentacles that the crabs utilise for defence.

CRABS HAVE A TAIL-LIKE abdomen similar to crayfish, but this is greatly reduced and folded under the body (cephalothorax). Female crabs can be distinguished from males by their much wider tail.

NATIVE SLATERS are found over most of Australia. The most common slater (*Porcellio scaber*) has been introduced from overseas and lives successfully in urban and suburban areas.

MOST SLATERS have wide, flattened bodies, but members of one group, called pill bugs, are able to roll into a ball when threatened. They look like short millipedes.

CRAYFISH CARRY THEIR EGGS underneath their tails. Rows of small appendages (called swimmerets) keep water moving over the eggs to maintain a high oxygen supply to the eggs.

Below: A Lamington Spiny Cray (*Euastacus sulcatus*) in its "threat" display.

Crustaceans are sometimes called the "insects of the sea" — they are the dominant invertebrates in the only environment that insects have not conquered. Most species live in the sea and the majority of the remainder live in fresh water, but there are also some species living successfully on land. They range in size from tiny water fleas, which are almost microscopic, to crabs that weigh as much as a small dog.

AS TOUGH AS BONE

Crustaceans are usually covered with a tough protective armour, a sort of crust, from which they derive their name. The armour has several layers, including a layer of calcium carbonate, which is the same substance that gives bone its toughness. Because the armour is not flexible, crustaceans need to shed their skins as they grow, in the same way that insects and spiders do. They need to find shelter during moulting, as the new shell is soft and flexible for a few hours afterwards to allow for an increase in size. The crustacean is particularly vulnerable to predators at this stage. A few species live as parasites in the bodies of other crustaceans and, therefore, do not need a tough covering.

Above: Hermit crabs may be common on tropical beaches. They are particularly active at night.

Right: Sea slaters are closely related to the more familiar species that live on land. This species lives on rocky shores.

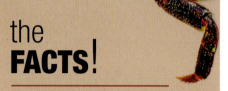

Above: Male fiddler crabs possess an oversized claw that is waved in a threatening manner at other male crabs.

THE BEST OF THE REST

Crabs, crayfish and prawns are the best known crustaceans in Australia, but there are a number of other groups of crustaceans that deserve attention. Shield shrimps appear in Australian deserts straight after rain, grow rapidly and swarm in their millions before dying out when the water dries up, leaving behind eggs that will stay dormant until the next rains.

Slaters are a group of crustaceans with a large number of marine species but include some that have moved onto land. They feed on decaying plant matter and fungi and can be found from forested areas to semi-arid regions. Landhoppers, sometimes known as "springtails", live under rocks and pot plants and are most commonly seen leaping into the air when uncovered. They are able to leap with a sudden flexing of the abdomen.

Centipedes & millipedes

ONE HUNDRED LEGS

The name centipede literally means "one hundred legs", but almost all Australian species have fewer than 100 legs. They can be separated from millipedes by having one pair of legs on each body segment. In all centipede species, the first pair of legs have been modified into a pair of poison claws, held under the head. These claws are attached to venom glands that are capable of paralysing and killing a large range of prey, mostly invertebrates such as insects and spiders. Although some Australian centipedes are quite large, bites to humans are rare and cause only local swelling and some irritation.

Above: This species belongs to a group of centipedes called scolopendrids. It is one of the largest in Australia.

Left: Millipedes tend to occur in moist, forested areas, living in leaf litter or under logs.

ONE THOUSAND LEGS

Millipedes differ from centipedes by having two pairs of legs on each segment. Very young millipedes have only one pair of legs per segment, and some hatchlings may have only three pairs of legs in total, making them difficult to tell apart from insects. All millipede species add more segments and legs at each moult until full size is achieved with adulthood. The name millipede literally means "one thousand legs", but no species' leg count comes even close to this figure.

MULTI-LEGGED COMPOSTERS

Unlike centipedes, millipedes are not carnivorous. Millipedes generally live in leaf litter or under logs, and feed on dead leaves, bark and rotting vegetable matter. They can be present in large numbers in some habitats and are very important in digesting organic material and turning it into rich soil to be used by plants.

A BITTER PILL

Some types of millipedes are able to defend themselves very successfully against predators. Each segment of the body has a pair of glands that produce a red or yellow fluid that can cause irritation to potential predators. These fluids may contain chemicals such as formic acid (used by ants to keep predators away) or hydrogen cyanide. They have a very bitter taste and can stain human skin — a severe stain can cause the skin to peel off.

Above, left: Pill millipedes are capable of rolling into a tight ball when threatened.

Above: Many millipedes possess a series of glands down the sides of the body that produce a highly irritating fluid.

the FACTS!

CENTIPEDES and millipedes are together known as myriapods, a name that means "many legs".

CENTIPEDES WILL CAPTURE and consume any prey they can overpower. They have been reported to kill frogs, geckoes and even mice.

THE LARGEST CENTIPEDES in Australia grow to 150 mm long. Overseas they may grow to 300 mm — as long as a school ruler.

CENTIPEDES ARE PREDATORS and in desert areas they will crawl down spider burrows to kill and eat spiders as large as tarantulas.

THE BITES of some centipedes from overseas are capable of causing serious illness.

ALL MILLIPEDES belonging to the order Polydesmida lack eyes and most are quite small. Some are less than 10 mm long as adults.

SOME FEMALE MILLIPEDES make elaborate egg-laying chambers. The chamber is made from dirt, cemented together with fluids from the millipede's anus.

Worms
— earthworms, leeches & others

Above: Earthworms feed on dead organic matter and are essential for adding nutrients and mixing different layers of soil.

The name "worm" covers a diverse group of unrelated invertebrates that range from quite simple animals to those whose bodies are very complex.

SOME OF THE SIMPLEST are flatworms, which include a great range of parasitic species. Land flatworms live under bark or logs in the moist regions of Australia. They are carnivorous, capturing prey by trapping it with mucus. Flatworms may grow up to 300 mm long.

LAND WORMS

Earthworms, leeches and marine worms all belong to the same phylum (Annelida). Their segmented bodies make them quite easy to distinguish from other worms, particularly when viewed close up. Earthworms live in soil and leaf litter and, because they lose water very easily, they are most common in wetter habitats. Earthworms feed on dead organic matter and break down material such as leaf litter to be later decomposed by bacteria. They also turn over the soil and, as such, are the driving force behind many ecosystems.

SEA WORMS

Marine worms are the largest group among the annelids, characterised by prominent tufts of hair or spines on the sides of the body. They are common in oceans around the world and many species build tubes made from sand cemented together with mucus. These tubes may make up a substantial proportion of coral reefs.

MISSING LINKS

Velvetworms (left) are perhaps the most remarkable invertebrates living today. They are a very ancient group and are sometimes seen as a link between worms and arthropods, having a long worm-like body and 14–16 pairs of clawed legs. The head has a pair of eyes, antennae and jaws from which a sticky fluid is produced to trap prey and deter predators.

Above: Flatworms are found in moist environments, particularly under logs.

BLOOD SUCKERS

Leeches are blood-sucking worms that feed on humans and other warm-blooded hosts. When a host is located, the leech makes an incision on the skin with three razor-sharp teeth and proceeds to feed. The leech injects a special digestive juice that keeps the blood flowing freely and which also works as an anaesthetic.

Above: Leeches feed on the blood of warm-blooded animals, including humans. They sometimes drop onto the host from overhead vegetation.

the FACTS!

FLATWORMS are often brightly coloured and patterned. They feed on slugs and earthworms and are sometimes found eating carrion.

THE LARGEST EARTHWORM in the world lives in Australia. The Giant Gippsland Earthworm (*Megascolides australis*) is found in south-east Victoria and can grow up to 3 m long.

VELVETWORMS have an unusual way of mating. The male deposits a packet of sperm onto the body of the female, which she then absorbs through the body wall. The sperm then travels through the body to fertilise the eggs.

ONCE A VELVETWORM TRAPS prey with its sticky fluid, it tears a hole in the body with its tough jaws and sucks out the insides.

FANWORMS LIVE in tubes on reefs. The head region is highly modified to include large fans of tentacles or gill filaments. These are designed to collect and sift plankton and passing organic matter.

LEECHES and earthworms are both male and female at the same time. This reproductive strategy is known as "hermaphroditism".

Slugs & snails
— mollusc minions

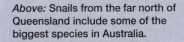

Above: Snails from the far north of Queensland include some of the biggest species in Australia.

Slugs and snails are part of a group of invertebrates called molluscs, the second largest group of animals on Earth behind the arthropods. Molluscs have soft bodies that are usually protected with a covering of hard shell. Although basically similar in their body designs, molluscs are remarkably diverse in size, shape and lifestyle. The main groups are snails and slugs, chitons, bivalves, and octopuses and squids.

BIVALVES, OCTOPUSES and squids are well known to most people, but chitons are much less so. They are an ancient group of molluscs that are common in rock pools and on rocky platforms between high and low tide. They range from 20–80 mm in length and have eight separate protective plates on their backs.

LAND-LUBBER MOLLUSCS

The snails and slugs, collectively called gastropods, have managed to survive very successfully on land. Their bodies are divided into a mass of organs in one half and a combined head and foot in the other. Some species have a shell that is secreted by the body wall surrounding the mass of organs and which therefore protects the most important part of the snail. However, the shell's greatest advantage is that it stops the snails drying out, enabling them to conquer land. Slugs manage to survive without shells, but, like many snails, they only live in the wetter parts of Australia and venture out most commonly after rain.

Above: The Red Triangle Slug (*Triboniophorus graeffei*) has a small "breathing hole" visible just inside one point of the triangle.

Right: Whelks and related snails are found close to the coast, particularly in mangrove areas.

Below: This rainforest snail has an incomplete shell. It is a transitional stage between snails and slugs.

the FACTS!

THE LARGEST invertebrate in the world is a giant squid that may grow to 14 m in length.

THE WORD gastropod literally means "stomach–foot".

MOLLUSCS RANGE IN SIZE from snails only a half a millimetre long to squids with a body length of many metres.

MOLLUSCS HAVE ALWAYS BEEN of interest to humans. Shellfish, octopuses and squids have been an important food source, shells are used for decoration and pearls made by oysters are used as jewellery.

SNAILS FURTHER PROTECT themselves from drying out by withdrawing completely into their shells and covering the entrance with a thick layer of slime that hardens to stop moisture passing through.

SNAILS AND SLUGS usually have two pairs of tentacles at the front of the head: an upper pair that bear the eyes and a lower pair that are used for touch. Both pairs can normally be retracted back into the head.

TOOTHY SPEARS & HARPOONS

Snails and slugs feed using a "radula", a tongue-like ribbon that is covered with rows of tiny teeth. The number of teeth ranges from fewer than twenty to more than 750,000. Herbivorous and scavenging gastropods use the radula to scrape algae from rocks, for example, whereas carnivorous species have the radula modified into a spear or dart. Some marine species, such as cone shells, also have venom glands associated with the harpoon-like radula. These can produce venom powerful enough to kill humans.

Conservation

Insects & spiders in danger
— threatened species & conservation

Below: The Ulysses Butterfly (*Papilio ulysses*) was once uncommon but is becoming more secure due to widespread planting of its host plants.

Native insects play an essential role in the ecology of all Australian environments and deserve our protection. Despite the apparent abundance of insects, they are not immune to human interference. Some species have already disappeared from the face of the Earth and others are currently being threatened with extinction by habitat destruction. Fortunately, awareness of the importance of insects is growing, and several species are now protected by law. By destroying insect species we break vital links in all food webs, which affects entire plant and animal communities, and, eventually, all humanity.

WHY BOTHER?

Given that many insect species are very common and may even cause problems to humans, the question of why we should protect insect species is often asked. There are several reasons:

- All animal species have a right to exist. Just as humans consider themselves important enough to continue to live and breed on Earth, all other species have the same rights.

- Insects are very useful to humans as tools for education and scientific research. The Vinegar Fly (*Drosophila melanogaster*) was one of the earliest and is still one of the best-studied animals in the world, particularly in the field of genetics.

Above: An Eltham Copper Butterfly caterpillar attended by ants at night. These butterflies are now more secure thanks to special reserves.

- Humans and all other animals rely on insects for food, either directly or indirectly. Plants rely on insects for nutrient recycling, seed dispersal and pollination. Without the insects that break down dead plants and animals, we would be up to our necks in rotting organic matter within a few years.

- Insects hold many of the keys to medical breakthroughs. "Bioprospecting" is the name given to the search for new compounds and medicines in the natural world. For example, insects were curing their own diseases with antibiotics millions of years before humans discovered them.

- Insects are good indicators of the health of the environment. Environmental scientists usually use insects as "indicator species" to assess the health of ecosystems on land and in freshwater habitats.

the FACTS!

THE EUROPEAN STAG BEETLE (*Lucanus cervus*) is protected by law in many parts of Europe and its trade is prohibited. It was once common over much of Europe but has disappeared from many areas due to agricultural pesticides.

PERHAPS THE RAREST BEETLE in the world is the Titan Longicorn (*Titanus giganteus*). To buy a specimen in 1914 when they were more common cost 2000 gold marks. Today a specimen would be worth many thousands of dollars.

IN THE USA, CONSERVATION programs for endangered birds cost, on average, 25 times more than programs for endangered insect species.

IT HAS BEEN ESTIMATED that 20% of all insects in North America are threatened by human activities.

WHERE ARE THE POLLINATORS?

Plants, including those eaten by humans, need pollinators in order to produce fruit and seeds successfully. The majority of the world's pollinators are insects (mostly bees, wasps and flies). In the last few decades, a number of factors, such as habitat destruction and the use of pesticides, have dramatically reduced the number of pollinators. This has caused some crops around the world to fail, putting farmers out of business and resulting in shortages of food. The same is probably occurring in natural ecosystems, but this is much more difficult to measure.

European Honeybees (*Apis mellifera*), the most widely used pollinators, are suffering from a range of diseases that have devastated their populations in some countries. Unfortunately, native bee species have also declined dramatically. This has led to "colony collapse disorder", where dozens of hives from a single apiary will literally disappear overnight.

Above: In north Queensland, the Cairns Birdwing Butterfly is returning to areas where it had disappeared due to loss of its food plant, *Aristolochia*.

THE TURNING TIDE

People around the world are becoming more aware of the importance of invertebrates to ecosystems and to us; international authorities (such as the International Union for the Conservation of Nature) are becoming more aware of the importance of protecting invertebrates; and zoos are becoming more aware of the importance and value of displaying invertebrate species.

In Papua New Guinea and parts of Asia and South America, butterflies are being farmed rather than being collected from the wild. Local people breed free-ranging butterflies for sale while protecting the native forests as a food source for the butterflies. Hundreds of Queensland school children belong to a program and have planted thousands of vines for the endangered Richmond Birdwing Butterfly (*Ornithoptera richmondia*). In Europe, butterfly, beetle and cricket species are being translocated into areas where they have become locally extinct.

Probably those conservation programs that are most successful are ones that remove the factors that threatened the insect species in the first place. If the main threats — such as habitat destruction or introduced pests — are removed, insect populations will often recover on their own. This is demonstrated by the recovery of the Lord Howe Island Stick Insect (*Dryococelus australis,* below).

the FACTS!

FRESHWATER INSECTS (such as dragonflies and mayflies) are threatened by pollution and the drying out of wetlands. In Australia, a number of stonefly species are listed as critically endangered.

THE FRIGATE ISLAND Giant Beetle (*Polposipus herculeanus*) lives only in dead trees on one small island in the Seychelles. It is almost extinct but is currently being reared in captivity at London Zoo.

HUMAN ACTIVITIES can have other indirect impacts on insect populations. In Hawaii, 85% of the parasitic insects that are devastating native butterflies were originally deliberately introduced to the islands to control pest moths.

EVEN ON THE ISLANDS around Antarctica, introduced pests are causing big problems to local insect species.

CONSERVATION of many threatened insects is difficult as we know nothing about their natural life histories, population levels or distribution. Often we do not know why populations are decreasing.

Left: An adult Lord Howe Island Stick Insect feeding on *Melaleuca*, the only food plant left to it in the wild.

Glossary

ABDOMEN The final section of the body of an invertebrate; the "belly".

ANTENNA One part of the paired sensory appendages on the heads of insects and some other invertebrates (plural – antennae).

ARACHNIDS A group of arthropods such as spiders and scorpions that all have two body parts and four pairs of legs.

ARANEOMORPH Advanced spiders whose fangs move sideways (horizontally). This group includes the majority of spiders.

ARTHROPODS Arthropods include insects, spiders and crustaceans. Phylum Arthropoda has been divided up, but joint-legged invertebrates with a body divided into segments are still referred to as arthropods.

BALLOONING Means of dispersal for spiderlings. (See page 61.)

BATESIAN MIMICRY When non-poisonous species mimic poisonous species and so get some protection from predators.

BUG General term for all insects and some other invertebrates. Technically it refers only to insects in the order Hemiptera.

CASTE System where social insects divide labour so that different forms of the same species perform different functions.

CEPHALOTHORAX Fused head and thorax of spiders.

CERCI Paired sense organs appended at the back of the abdomen of some insects.

CHELICERAE First pair of appendages in spiders: short, thick and holding the fangs.

CHITIN Tough, water-resistant outer layer of invertebrates' exoskeleton.

CRIBELLUM Sieve-like plate covering the spinnerets at the end of "cribellate" spiders' abdomens; produces thick, fuzzy silk.

ECHOLOCATION Sensing objects by sending out sounds then analysing echoes reflected after they impact.

ELAIOSOME Soft, fleshy structure on plant seeds that is attractive to ants.

EXOSKELETON Tough outer covering of insects, literally an external skeleton.

EYESPOT Coloured spot like an eye on butterfly or moth wings: frightens predators.

FAMILY Group of closely related genera.

FLANGE A rim, edge or flap that sticks out from the body of some animals.

GALL Plant outgrowth, usually on the stem, which is caused by insects, mites or fungi.

GENUS Group of closely related species (pl. — genera).

HEMIMETABOLA Insects that don't metamorphose between immature and adult stages (adj.— hemimetabolous).

HOLOMETABOLA Insects that metamorphose (pupate) between immature and adult stages (adj. — holometabolous).

HONEYDEW Sugar-rich liquid produced by sap-sucking insects.

HYPERPARASITES Parasite that develops in another parasite species' body.

INQUILINE Animal that lives in the nest or home of another species — most commonly insects living in ant or termite nests.

INVERTEBRATES Animals with no backbone: they make up ≈ 98% of animal species.

LARVA Immature holometabolous insect: one that metamorphoses (pupates) to become an adult (plural – larvae).

MANDIBLES Main parts of an insect's mouthparts, usually designed for chewing.

METAMORPHOSIS Process of immature insect (e.g. caterpillar) transforming into an adult (e.g. butterfly), sometimes in a cocoon.

MIMICRY Where a species resembles another to its own advantage.

MIMICRY COMPLEX Group of species, often unrelated and usually poisonous, that mimic each other. Once predators encounter one member, all members are protected.

MOULT Skin-shedding by arachnids, insects and crustaceans as they grow.

MOULTING FLUID Fluid that helps break down old skin and separate it from the new at the beginning of the moult.

MULLERIAN MIMICRY The mimicking of another poisonous species to deter predators.

MUTUALISM Interaction between two species that benefits both.

MYGALOMORPH Primitive, mostly ground-dwelling spiders: the fangs move up and down (vertically).

NYMPH Immature hemimetabolous insect: moults directly into an adult without metamorphosis (e.g. dragonflies).

OCELLI Simple additional eyes on insects (sing. — ocellus).

OMMATIDIUM Single facet of compound eyes of insects.

OOTHECA Tough egg case of mantids and cockroaches (pl. — oothecae).

ORDER Group of closely related families.

OSMETERIUM Soft, forked organ that appears behind heads of some caterpillars (Papilionidae or swallowtails): usually strong smelling and is used for defence.

OVERWINTERING Like hibernation: insects or spiders pass winter with little or no activity.

OVIPOSITOR Long tube on some insects' abdomens used to lay eggs. It is modified into a sting in many ants, bees and wasps.

PAEDOGENESIS Reproduction by an insect before it becomes an adult.

PALPS Segmented head appendages used to manipulate food. Called pedipalps in spiders, used as antennae; also hold male sex organs.

PARASITE Animal completely dependent on another animal's body for food; usually feeds without killing the host.

PARASITOID Develops entirely in a single host insect's body and eventually kills it.

PARTHENOGENESIS Ability to reproduce without eggs being fertilised by sperm.

PATHOGEN Parasite that causes disease.

PHEROMONES Chemical smell from one animal that influences behaviour of others of the same species, usually for mating.

PHORESY Transportation of one species by another (also called hitchhiking).

POLLINIA Mass of pollen grains transferred as a single unit in pollination (sing. — pollinium).

POLYEMBRYONY Where two or more embryos develop from one fertilised egg.

PROBOSCIS Tubular organ comprised of fused mouthparts used to suck up liquid food.

PROLEGS Fleshy legs along caterpillars' bodies: differ from true legs behind the head.

PUPA Non-feeding stage of holometabolous insects between larva and adult.

RADULA Mollusc's "tongue": usually tough, horny ribbon, covered with microscopic teeth.

SCOLI Outgrowth from caterpillar's body wall, often branched or bearing hairs.

SPECIES Type or kind of animal or plant: generally defined as being unable to breed with other types.

SPIGOTS Tiny, valve-like glands that make up spiders' spinnerets. Each is attached to a silk gland. They control silk production.

SPINNERETS Organs used to produce silk: found in spiders' abdomens; below caterpillars' heads; on other appendages of other insects.

SPIRACLE External opening of the trachea, the breathing system of insects and other invertebrates.

STABILIMENTUM Broad ribbons of thick silk, usually a cross or circle, spun in the centre of a spider's web.

STARTLE DISPLAY Alarm response in many animal species, particularly insects. Eyespots or warning colours are flashed in response to disturbance, in an effort to deter predators.

STRIDULATION The sound that insects produce by rubbing hard projections on the body against a file-like body surface.

SUBSOCIAL BEHAVIOUR Range of group behaviours (e.g. parental care) with increasing levels of complexity, leading to coordinated social behaviour.

THORAX Middle section of an insect, between the head and abdomen: usually bears three pairs of legs and two pairs of wings.

TRACHEA Respiratory tubes stretching from the outer spiracles to the internal organs of insects and other invertebrates.

TYMBAL Sound-producing membranes in male cicadas' abdomens. They are clicked rapidly in and out to produce sound.

VERTEBRATES Animals with backbones.

Web links & further reading

WEBSITES

CSIRO Entomology:
http://www.csiro.au/org/Entomology.html

Australian Museum Online:
http://www.amonline.net.au

Australian Entomological Society:
http://www.agric.nsw.gov.au/Hort/ascu/myrmecia/society.htm

University of Southern Queensland, Find-a-spider Guide:
http://www.usq.edu.au/spider/index.htm

AUSTRALIAN MUSEUMS

Australian Museum: www.austmus.gov.au

Qld — www.qm.qld.gov.au

WA — www.museum.wa.gov.au

SA — www.samuseum.sa.gov.au

Vic — http://museumvictoria.com.au

Tas — www.tmag.tas.gov.au

NT — www.nt.gov.au/nreta/museums/index.html

PUBLICATIONS

Berenbaum, M.R. *Bugs in the System: Insects and Their Impact on Human Affairs*, Addison-Wesley Publishing Company, USA, 1995

Edwards, P.J. and Wratten, S.D. *Ecology of Insect–Plant Interactions*, Edward Arnold Publishing Ltd, UK, 1980

Hawkeswood, T. *Beetles of Australia*, Angus & Robertson Publishers, NSW, 1981

Klausnitzer, B. *Beetles*, Exeter Books, USA, 1983

Macquitty, M. and Mound, L. *Megabugs: The Natural History Museum Book of Insects*, Carlton Books, UK, 1995

Matthews, E.G. *A Guide to the Genera of Beetles of South Australia (Part 2)*, South Australian Museum, Adelaide, 1982

Matthews, E.G. and Kitching, R.L. *Insect Ecology*, University of Queensland Press, Brisbane, Qld, 1976

Meglitsch, P.A. and Schram F.R. *Invertebrate Zoology (3rd ed.)*, Oxford University Press, New York, 1991

Naumann, I.D. (Ed.) The *Insects of Australia*, Melbourne University Press, Melbourne, 1991

New, T.R. *Insects as Predators*, New South Wales University Press, Sydney, 1991

New, T.R. *Introductory Entomology for Australian Students*, New South Wales University Press, Sydney, 1992

O'Toole, C. *Insects in Camera: A Photographic Essay on Behaviour*, Oxford University Press, UK, 1985

Preston-Mafham, K. *Bugs and Beetles*, New Burlington Books, UK, 1997

Preston-Mafham, R. *The Book of Spiders and Scorpions*, Crescent Books, USA, 1991

Preston-Mafham, K. and Preston-Mafham, R. *The Natural World of Bugs and Insects*, PRC Publishing, UK, 2000

Rentz, D.C.F. et al. *A Guide to Australian Grasshoppers and Locusts*, Natural History Publications, Borneo, 2003

Tweedie, M. *Encyclopedia of Insects and Arachnids*, Octopus Books Ltd, UK, 1975

Waldbauer, G. *The Handy Bug Answer Book*, Visible Ink Press, USA, 1998

Wangberg, J.K. *Six-Legged Sex: The Erotic Lives of Bugs*, Fulcrum Publishing, USA, 2001

Index

A
Acilius spp. 42
Acrophylla titan 23
Albatross, Common 4
alderflies 44
Amegilla sp. 15
Amitermes meridionalis 45
Anoplognathus spp. 55
Ant
  African Driver 38
  Blue 4, 16, 35
  bull 6, 51, 52
  desert 55
  harvester 14
  honeypot 55
  jumping 50
  Jumping Jack 51
  meat 47
  sugar 14
  Velvet 16
Antarctica 77
Antherophagus spp. 42
antlions 45
  Giant Antlion Lacewing 28
aphids 14, 24, 25, 34, 36, 47, 50
Apis mellifera 15, 46, 56, 77
arachnids 3, 6, 58, 71, 79
Arachnura sp. 68
araneomorphs 63
Argiope keyserlingi 69
Aristolochia spp. 77
arthropods 5, 74, 75, 79
Aspidomorpha spp. 53
Atrax robustus 20, 63
Austracantha minax 68
Austrolestes spp. 41

B
backswimmers 24, 44
bacteria 56, 74
  foulbrood 56
  honeybee paralysis 56
Badumna insignis 65–67
Batocera wallacei 19
bats 13, 40, 43, 56
Bee
  Blue Banded 15
  Bumble 15
  carpenter 15
  cuckoo 15
  European Honey 15, 46, 49, 56
  mason 15
  native 15, 77
  Teddy Bear 15
Beetle 6, 7, 8, 9, 34, 55
  ambrosia 47
  bombardier 52, 53
  burying 7
  byrrhid 52
  checkered 33
  Christmas 19, 37, 55
  Darkling 52
  death-watch 54
  Devil's Coach-horse 50
  diving 42, 44
  Egyptian 37
  European Stag 76
  Feather-winged 19
  fireflies 54
  Frigate Island Giant 77
  Great Water 53
  hydraenid 44
  jewel 18, 19, 40, 41
  leaf 6, 19, 35, 36
  Longicorn 18, 19, 41, 57, 76
    Titan 76
    Wallace's 19
  mahout 7
  passalid 18, 46
  paussid 50
  pie-dish 55
  ptilid 57
  Radar 40
  rhinoceros 7, 18, 38
  rhipicerid 40
  rhipiphorid 18
  rove 18
  scarab 19, 40, 56
  Sexton 7
  silken fungus 42
  Spanish Fly 53
  spercheid 44
  Spiny Leaf 52
  stag 18, 19
  tenebrionid 52
  tiger 51
  tortoise 19, 41, 53
  tumbling flower 40
  water 44
  water boatmen 24, 44
  Water Penny 44
  whirligig 40, 44
birds 6, 10, 22, 33, 51, 53, 55, 56, 59
bivalves 75
Blaps polychresta 37
Bombyx mori 13
Brachynus spp. 53
Brachypsectra spp. 50
bristletails 7, 30, 31
Brontoscorpio anglicus 6
Bug 7, 8, 30
  assassin 24, 25, 50, 51
  bed 24
  Beekiller Assassin 30
  Bronze Orange 30, 52
  creeping water 44
  Crusader 25
  eurymelid 24, 47
  Feather-legged Assassin 50, 51
  Green Vegetable 25
  Harlequin 39
  jewel 24, 41
  leafhopper 32
  lygaeid 25
  pill 72
  pyrrhocorid 6
  shield 6, 24, 25, 39
  spit 25
  stink 24
  toad 44
  true 6, 24, 25
Butterfly 10–13, 29, 30, 32, 34, 41, 43, 49, 53, 76–77
  Australian Leafwing 10
  Blue-banded Eggfly 11
  Cabbage White 11
  Caper White 10
  Common Brown 53
  Common Eggfly 10, 11
  Common Imperial Blue 10, 47, 53
  Cruiser 39, 53
  Dainty Swallowtail 43
  Eltham Copper 76
  Glasswing 46
  Lesser Wanderer 11, 33
  Lurcher 11
  lycaenid 47
  Monarch (see Wanderer)
  Orchard 8, 30, 31, 38, 43, 52, 54, 55
  Birdwing
    Cairns 6, 10, 11, 49, 53, 77
    Queen Alexandra 11
    Richmond 77
  Skipper 11
  Southern Sedge-darter 10
  Ulysses 10, 11, 41, 76
  Viceroy 33
  Wanderer 10, 11, 33, 39, 48

C
caddisflies 7, 28, 44, 51
Caedicia olivacea 41
Caliroa cerasi 39
caterpillars 6, 7, 9–12, 16, 28, 30, 32–35, 42, 45, 47, 52, 53, 56, 57, 64, 76, 79
Celaenia kinbergi 59, 67
centipedes 3, 4, 5, 14, 55, 56, 60, 73
  scolopendrid 73
Cephonodes kingii 13
Cethosia penthesilea 11, 78
Charidotella sexpunctata 41
Cheiracanthium spp. 65
chitons 75
Chortoicetes terminifera 7, 55
Chrysoperla sp. 50
Cicada 9, 24, 25, 54, 79
  Bladder 25, 54
  Double Drummer 24
  Greengrocer 25, 31, 40
  Yellow Monday 25
Clubiona robusta 65
cockchafers 40
Cockroach 6, 7, 18, 27, 30, 39, 40, 42, 55, 64
  American 40
  Giant Burrowing 54, 57
Corinnidae 64
Coscinocera hercules 12, 38
crabs 4, 72
  fiddler 72
  ghost 4
craneflies 20
crayfish 4, 5, 72
Creophilus sp. 50
Cricket 26, 31, 42, 54
  Black Field 55
  field 26
  humpbacked 26
  king 26
  mole 17, 26, 35, 54
  raspy 26
  Spiny Tree 26
Crow, Australian 4
Cyclochila australasiae 25, 31, 41, 54
Cystosoma saundersii 25

D
damselflies 2, 21, 41, 44, 50, 54
Danaus
  chrysippus 11
  plexippus 11, 39, 48
Deinopis subrufa 59
Diamma bicolor 4, 16
Dicopomorpha echmepterygis 57
Dineutes politus 40
dinosaurs 6, 29
diplurans 7
diseases 20, 24, 37, 56, 76, 77
dobsonflies 7
Doleschallia bisaltide 10
Dolomedes spp. 59
Dolophones sp. 59
Doratifera spp. 13
  vulnerans 39, 42
Dorylus wilverthi 38
Dragonfly 7, 30, 42, 43, 44, 50, 54, 57, 77
  Baron 21, 40
Drosophila melanogaster 76
Dytiscus sp. 53

E
earthworm (see worms)
earwigs 9, 18, 27, 52
Echidna 56
Eggfly
  Blue-banded 11
  Common 10, 11
  Danaid 33
Encara floccosum 52
Entomophthora muscae 56
Epiphyas postvittana 13
Eriophora transmarina 62, 69
Eurychora sp. 52
Eurycnema goliath 23, 53
Extatosoma tiaratum 23

F
fish 21, 27, 50, 53, 59
fleas 34, 43
Fly 7, 20, 31, 34, 35
  blackflies 20
  blowflies 20, 37, 50
  Bush 20, 31, 56
  flesh 20
  fruit 62
  Giant Robber 20
  house 20
  Louse 38
  march 34
  robber 50
  Scuttle 7
  Tsetse 39
  wallaby 35
  Vinegar 76
Flower Beetle
  Two-Spotted 39
frogs 22, 29, 50, 73
fungi 19, 56, 72, 79

G
Gasteracantha fornicata 69
gastropods 75
Geolycosa godeffroyi 60, 64
Gnaphosidae 64
Graphognathus leucoloma 39
Grasshoppers 7, 8, 18, 25, 26, 30, 42, 78
  Giant 57
Gryllotalpa spp. 54
Gull, Australian 4

H
Halobates spp. 24
Helpis minitabunda 70
Hemicloea sp. 64
Heoclisis fulva 28
Heteronympha merope 53
Hickmania troglodytes 63
Hierodula spp. 22
Hippobosca variegata 38
Hippodamia convergens 29
Hispellinus sp. 52
hypochilomorphs 63
Hypolimnas
  alimena 11
  bolina 11

I
Icerya purchasi 39
Iridomyrmex cordatus 47

J
Jalmenus evagoras 10, 47, 53

K
katydids 9, 26, 32, 57
  Green 41
  Prickly 52

L
Lacewing 7, 18, 39, 43
  Giant Antlion (see antlions)
  Green 50
  mantispid 28, 51
  Orange 11, 78
  Red 4
ladybirds 18, 19, 29, 50, 53
Lampona cylindrata 65
landhoppers 72
Latrodectus hasselti 67
Leafhopper 24, 32
  Green 25
leaf insects 23
Leopard 4
Leptops sp. 18
lerp insects 24, 45
Lethocerus insulanus 24
lice 7, 34
lizards 51
locusts 25, 26
  Australian Plague Locust 7, 55
Lucanus cervus 76
Lycosa forresti 64
Lytta vesicatoria 53

M
Macropanesthia rhinoceros 54
Malachius bipustulatus 39
Mantid 7, 18, 22, 30, 32, 50
  amorphoscelid 22
  Giant 51
  Green 22, 32, 53
  Netwinged 22
  praying 8, 35
Maratus volans 70
mayflies 7, 27, 31, 44, 55, 77
mealybugs 25
Megacrania batesii 23
Megascolides australis 74
Megaselia scalaris 7
Melaleuca spp. 77
Melanophila acuminata 40
midges 20
  fungus 51
millipedes 3, 4, 5, 72, 73
mites 3, 4, 5, 71, 79
Miturga sp. 65
molluscs 5, 44, 75
Mopsus mormon 70
Mordella spp. 40
mosquitoes 8, 20, 24, 43
Moth 8–9, 12–13, 30, 32–34, 40, 43, 57, 68
  arctiid 53
  Bee 13
  Cup 13, 42
    Mottled 39
  Emperor Gum 53
  geometrid 32
  ghost 38
  Hawk 12, 13, 33
    Madagascar 12
  Hercules 12, 33, 38, 40, 42
  Light Brown Apple 13
  looper 32
  Relict Braconid 17
  Saunder's Case 45
  tiger 13, 33
  White Stemmed Gum 53
Musca vetustissima 20, 31, 56
Musgraveia sulciventris 52
mygalomorphs 3, 63
Myrmarachne spp. 59, 70
Myrmecia spp. 14, 51

N
Nanosella fungi 19
Nephila sp. 62, 69
  ornata 59, 60
Nezara viridula 25
Numbat 56

O
octopus 75
Ocymyrmex spp. 55
Oecophylla smaragdina 14, 45, 51
Oiketicus elongatus 45
Ordgarius monstrosus 59
Ornithoptera
  alexandrae 11
  priamus 10, 11
  richmondia 77
Orthodera ministralis 22, 53